To Pastor Gordon and Pam,

I pray this book would in someway encourage you, just as you encourage many others.

Grace and peace,

Christin

*How Jesus is the greatest man to ever live
and how we can live like him.*

ALL MAN

ALL AMAZING

CHRISTIAN BALLENGER

Print ISBN: 978-1-09837-768-7
Ebook ISBN: 978-1-09837-769-4

Cover Design: Koko Toyama
Printed in the United States

To Heidi and Marshall, the greatest gifts a man can be given.
Thank you for trusting me to lead like Jesus and giving me the daily
privilege of experiencing him through your love.

CONTENTS

PREFACE

I have a love/hate relationship with running.

As a kid, this relationship was definitely more hate than love. Just the thought of it made me tired, so you can imagine my reluctance to do so at the time. Gym class was definitely not among my favorites, as I was not very athletic. In anything involving running, I was almost always slated last.

Growing up in the inner city, though, you had to be able to run. At a moment's notice, you could be in the wrong place at the wrong time. On one occasion, a neighbor's Rottweiler broke free and started chasing me and my cousin around the neighborhood; this, hands down, is the fastest I have ever run. Of course, the oh too recognizable sound of a gunshot always prompted the immediate reaction to flee.

Running, for me, was something steeped in emotion - either fatigue or fear.

Now, I see running a little differently. As an adult, it has become one of the main ways I renew myself physically, though I much prefer a treadmill than terrain. However, no matter what time of the day I go to the gym, I have observed one thing without fail - I am *never* running alone.

On one level, I think all of us adults see the utility of running, whether we like to or not. Yes, it benefits our health and adds to our well-being but it is more than this. Could it be that we each recognize running as a metaphor for the lives each of us are to live? In this way, I would say they are less like a sprint and more like *The Amazing Race*.

If this is the case, we have all seen people not run very well. As a young man, in the absence of a father, I searched for a man whose example would inform and inspire how I was to run. While there were those who surely impacted and even helped shape my life, I must confess that my search was left unfulfilled. Between lapses in integrity, alcohol addiction, immoral lifestyles and divorce, my affection for these men was not enough for me to allow them to cross a certain threshold of influence.

Life is certainly a lot of things but I would not describe it as easy to navigate. Now that I am a father myself, I aspire to be the best dad possible. I realize, however, despite my most sincere efforts, I will not truly be able to teach my son to run without clear and reliable directions. Where do I get these directions? Where does any of us?

If we're going to run an amazing race, we need someone to help us who is indeed *amazing*. While there may be a lack of those we can follow, there is one person who fits the bill: Jesus Christ. As we embark on the journey through his extraordinary life, I pray the pages of this book would provide an assurance that this answer is, indeed, sufficient.

Truly, Jesus is *All Man All Amazing*.

"AN AMAZING INTRODUCTION" – JESUS IS GOD...AND MAN

Philippians 2:5-8

> [5]*In your relationships with one another, have the same mindset as Christ Jesus:*
>
> [6]*Who, being in very nature God,*
>
> *did not consider equality with God something*
>
> *to be used to his own advantage;*
>
> [7]*rather, he made himself nothing*
>
> *by taking the very nature of a servant,*
>
> *being made in human likeness.*
>
> [8]*And being found in appearance as a man,*
>
> *he humbled himself*
>
> *by becoming obedient to death—*
>
> *even death on a cross!*

Amazing.

This is a word we have become quite accustomed to using. How often though do we stop to think about what it really means?

Amazing has been defined as "causing astonishment, great wonder, or surprise."[1]

Now, not all surprises are good. We all have had instances where we received bad news we were not expecting, like an unfavorable medical diagnosis or the death of a family member. I must admit, at my core, I do not even really like surprises. This is probably most telling from an episode early on in my marriage. My wife, Heidi, whom I love and cherish, devised a grand plan to throw a surprise birthday party for me at a restaurant I had been raving about. Unfortunately for her (and my guests), I foiled that plan. On the day she had intended on us celebrating, she was instead calling all of our friends to tell them the party would no longer be happening. Me not wanting to take an unplanned long drive, and my bad attitude to boot, were the reasons for the cancellation – I will never live that one down.

Even for me, there have been times in my life where I have been *pleasantly* surprised. One standout instance actually involves my wife's grandmother. Preparing to spend Christmas with my in-laws, a discussion started amongst the family about the holiday menu. As it turns out, Heidi's family praised her grandmother for her famous fried chicken, which made it to the list. Now, I like to think of myself as a fried chicken aficionado, so my expectations were somewhat mild. After sitting at the dinner table and taking one bite of her chicken, I can honestly say that it was the best chicken I've ever had. Not bad for a 93-year old!

The greatest surprise of my life came on June 7, 2019. Heidi and I decided not to find out the gender of our first child. For months, I was convinced we were having a girl; to this day, I am not even sure why. When the time came for the baby to be born, though I was proved wrong, I have never been more thrilled to have been so. Our son, Marshall, was born that day. Not only was I surprised but also one might say "astonished" and full of "wonder," as I marveled at the miracle of his birth. Surely, this is what the dictionary writer had in mind when defining the word "amazing."

---

1   https://www.merriam-webster.com/dictionary/amazing

When reflecting on the opening words from the apostle Paul, I wonder if my use – our use – of this word is even sufficient? In his first century letter to Christians living in the city of Philippi, Paul describes something that is *truly amazing*. The gravity of these words is both worthy of stopping and starting the presses. In Jesus Christ, the architect of the universe, creator of heaven and earth, the omniscient, omnipresent, omnipotent God became...a man.

We should not confuse this God-man with, let's say, the likes of the Greek hero, Heracles (better known by his Roman alias, "Hercules").[2] For starters, Jesus is not the product of mythology. History attests to Jesus' existence and suggesting he did not walk the earth would mean largely discrediting it. Moreover, even according to this legend, Heracles is half man/half divine. Jesus, however, is not half anything.

Though any description of a God like this will never be totally sufficient, theologians have described Christ's humanity and divinity by using the term, "hypostatic union." This expression simply means he is *"fully God and fully man."* In Christ, these two natures are united, not divided, in one person.[3]

My son, Marshall, is the product of two parents of a different race. While Heidi is as Caucasian as they come, I happen to be African American. You could imagine, then, that Marshall takes on mixed features, half of which come from me and the other half from his mother (even though he is very light-skinned). One day, he may be filling out a college application and specify that he is half Black and half White.

The hypostatic union, however, is not like a mixed child. It is not like a coin with two halves. We should, instead, think more along the lines of *H2O*. Both hydrogen and oxygen combine to form what we know as *water*. It is an essential, life-giving resource, created as a result of two elements

---

2   Heracles. (2021, February 09). Retrieved March 11, 2021, from https://www.britannica.com/topic/Heracles

3   Mathis, D. (2021, March 10). What is THE HYPOSTATIC UNION? Retrieved March 11, 2021, from https://www.desiringgod.org/articles/what-is-the-hypostatic-union

merging to form this chemical compound. Though the molecular structure of this substance is a simple formula, its physical and chemical properties are actually "extraordinarily complicated."[4] How else could you explain water's ability to take on solid, liquid and gas form? Maybe what is even harder to explain is how water in its solid form, ice, is less dense than its liquid form; this is why ice floats.

In Jesus Christ, both God and man have merged to form something like none other. Although this union is "extraordinarily complicated," the existence of Jesus is essential, and he gives life to all who come to him. The intent is not for us to rack our brains trying to determine how a man can walk on water but to marvel at the one in whom this was possible. Though Jesus is "all man," he is also, unequivocally, "all God." Of course, our discussion is centered on the humanity of Jesus but this cannot be divorced from his divinity. After clearly establishing this at the onset, we will have the freedom to focus on the human life of our Lord.

---

4   Zumdahl, S. S. (2021, February 02). Water. Retrieved March 11, 2021, from https://www.britannica.com/science/water

PART 1-

ALL GOD

There are many who have been deemed, have themselves espoused, or better yet have *tried*, to be God over the course of history. Whether the Egyptian pharaohs of old,[5] the Caesars of Rome[6] or even Jim Jones,[7] these claims of deity have certainly left us wanting. Is Jesus any different?

IN THE BEGINNING

Have you ever heard the expression, "I have been doing this since you were in diapers?" While new up-and-comers have vied for the position of "God," Jesus is the one who has steadily held on to this title, and it does not appear he is at all in danger of losing it. Indeed, his reign has spanned civilizations, empires and regimes, even dating back to the earliest on record.[8]

Jesus has been around since the beginning. Which beginning you may ask?

---

5   Pharaoh. (1998, July 20). Retrieved March 11, 2021, from https://www.britannica.com/topic/pharaoh

6   Grant, M. (1999, July 26). Augustus. Retrieved March 11, 2021, from https://www.britannica.com/biography/Augustus-Roman-emperor

7   Carter, J. (2018, November 14). 9 things you should know About Jim Jones and the Jonestown Massacre. Retrieved March 11, 2021, from https://www.thegospelcoalition.org/article/9-things-know-jim-jones-jonestown-massacre/

8   Frye, R. N. (2000, February 05). History of Mesopotamia. Retrieved March 11, 2021, from https://www.britannica.com/place/Mesopotamia-historical-region-Asia

Is it the beginning of Western culture?

Much before.

Is it, then, the beginning of the Church?

Way earlier.

Is it simply the beginning of organized religion?

Not even close.

Jesus has been around since *our beginning*. This is what John the apostle seemed to think anyway.

> [1]*In the beginning was the Word, and the Word was with God, and the Word was God.* [2]*He was with God in the beginning.* [3]*Through him all things were made; without him nothing was made that has been made.*
>
> [14]*The Word became flesh and made his dwelling among us. We have seen his glory, the glory of the one and only Son, who came from the Father, full of grace and truth.* (John 1:1-3, 14)

The apostle John walked with Jesus, talked with Jesus, ate with Jesus and was a witness to the amazing life he lived. Impressed by just how amazing this life was, he was compelled to employ his pen to convey this to others. In doing so, he makes plain his purpose for writing:

> [30]*Jesus performed many other signs in the presence of his disciples, which are not recorded in this book.* [31]*But these are written that you may believe that Jesus is the Messiah, the Son of God, and that by believing you may have life in his name.* (John 20:30-31)

John writes in order for his readers to walk away with a clear sense of Jesus' identity, namely that he is the Messiah (a divine king), the Son of God. He tells of his unparalleled wisdom, miracles and love, which is the greatest ever known (John 15:13). John concedes to not covering nearly all of the things Jesus did. In fact, he suggests that all the authors in the world could not exhaust the details of Jesus' life if they were to write about him (John 21:25) – including this one.

Realizing this, he carefully selects material in order to achieve his goal, wasting no time establishing Jesus' divine nature. He begins by saying, "In the beginning . . ." John leaves no room for suggestion when it comes to the person of Jesus. The Son of God is not a newcomer, nor did he one day suddenly come to exist. Based on what John writes at the onset of his gospel, though, he is the reason why everything else did.

The first description we see of Jesus in John's gospel is, "the Word." In Koine Greek, the original language of John and the other New Testament writers, this denotes "a *word*, being the expression of a *thought*; a saying. [This] is preeminently used of *Christ* (Jn 1:1), expressing the *thoughts* of the Father through the Spirit."[9] When we accept that God exists in three persons – Father, Son and Holy Spirit – we understand how *the Word* was both "with God" and "was God" in the beginning.

As things were being created, the thoughts of the Father were expressed by the Word and through the Spirit. The book of Genesis echoes these sentiments in its opening remarks:

> [1]*In the beginning God created the heavens and the earth.* [2]*Now the earth was formless and empty, darkness was over the surface of the deep, and the Spirit of God was hovering over the waters.* [3]*And God said, "Let there be light," and there was light.* (Genesis 1:1-3)

If you continue reading in Genesis 1, you will see God did a lot of speaking as he was establishing the heavens and the earth. Truly, without *the Word*, "nothing was made that has been made." God's first recorded words resulted in light coming into being. John highlights the significance of this

---

9   HELPS Word-Studies, "lógos"

when he says, "In him was life, and that life was the light of all mankind" (John 1:4). As essential as water is to life, light is just as essential.[10] In the beginning, the Spirit of God may have been hovering over the waters but God saw fit for light to be the hallmark of his creative process. Moreover, as an expression of the very thought of light from the Father, Jesus carries light within himself; he is truly able to grant life in his name. He is the light that overcomes darkness.

If you're like me, there are times when you walk into a room and do not want to turn on the light. At the top of my list is during the middle of the night when a baby, who should be sleeping, wakes up for any number of reasons. I try to do everything I can to maintain the aura of sleep, for both our sakes. This, however, gets a little tricky when needing to change a diaper.

Though turning on a light in a room inherently makes things easier, having a switch on the wall means it is optional. Similarly, when Jesus stepped into history, not everyone was to receive him. To highlight the great need for the light of Christ, a forerunner was selected: John the Baptist.

> [6]*There was a man sent from God whose name was John.* [7]*He came as a witness to testify concerning that light, so that through him all might believe.* [8]*He himself was not the light; he came only as a witness to the light.* (John 1:6-8)

John the Baptist was a man sent by God. This was so acknowledged in his day that his contemporaries actually thought he was the Messiah (John 1:20). In order for the readers of his gospel to not make this same mistake, John the apostle clarifies that "He himself was not the light; he came only as a witness to the light" (John 1:8). Indeed, the world's most famous baptizer was a means to a divine end, thus pointing people to the light that was coming into the world. Both Johns, then, share the same goal: being witnesses to the light that all might believe.

---

10   Stark, G. (1999, July 26). Light. Retrieved March 11, 2021, from https://www.britannica.com/science/light

I like to think of John the Baptist's ministry as a good movie trailer. Each of us at some point in time has gone to see a movie, in large part because of the trailer. You may have even been in the theater to see a different film, when one of the previews caught your eye. While I will admit that the trailer is sometimes better than the actual film, this is hardly the case with John and Jesus.

There was such a buzz generated by John. For the first time in a long time God was speaking to his chosen people, the Jews. Though they were excited by the presence of this peculiar prophet, listening to his entire message revealed he was only the trailer, not the actual film. He says, "This is the one I spoke about when I said, 'He who comes after me has surpassed me because he was before me'" (John 1:15). Just like a movie has to be shot first for the trailer to be created, John the Baptist is clear to point out that Jesus existed *before* him. This is not a reference to birth order, as Luke's gospel tells us John was *born* prior to Jesus (see Luke, chapters one and two). What our baptizer friend is saying is that Jesus is the Preeminent One, who existed prior to him and the rest of humanity.

Despite the efforts of John the Baptist, there were those who would not receive the light. Even though Jesus' light produced life in the beginning, and still does so until this day, he was not recognized. There were those, however, who did receive him.

What, though, did it mean for Jesus to be received?

Those who received Jesus acknowledged that in him *the Word* had become *flesh* and made his dwelling among them. That's right, for the first time in history the claims of a man saying he was God were actually true. There was a living, breathing God in their midst whose glory they beheld. This was a glory that surpassed the temple, the Law of Moses and, yes, John the Baptist – all a really big deal to any first century Jew. This Jesus, who was himself God and in closest relationship with the Father, was making the true God known by his flesh and bone presence among the people of his day.

Let's not just take the apostle John's word for it, though.

NOTORIOUS

Perhaps one of the greatest evidences for the authenticity of Christianity is the testimony of Paul.

We know him as the most prolific writer in the New Testament. Most modern weddings probably feature some form of his literature, especially his well-known poem regarding love (see 1 Corinthians 13). What cannot be ignored, though, is his infamy for being one of the greatest early opponents to the Jesus movement.

Paul, who was born "Saul" in the influential city of Tarsus, was a man of devastating loyalty. He held firm to his convictions and would go to great lengths to uphold them. He describes himself in a letter to the Philippians:

> *If anyone else thinks he has reason for confidence in the flesh,*
> *I have more: ⁵circumcised on the eighth day, of the people of*
> *Israel, of the tribe of Benjamin, a Hebrew of Hebrews; as to*
> *the law, a Pharisee; ⁶as to zeal, a persecutor of the church; as*
> *to righteousness under the law, blameless.* (Philippians 3:4b-6)

Paul makes it clear that his loyalties did not always lie with the church. In fact, not only did he deem it insufficient to simply continue to be dedicated to his way of life, he also found it necessary to extinguish the church once-and-for-all. There was no doubt in his mind that this Jesus, and those who followed him, was a threat to all he knew and loved. How could he allow the tradition, culture and faith of his ancestors to be eradicated, seemingly overnight, by a sect claiming a Galilean rabbi – often at odds with Israel's teachers – had somehow risen from the dead? Even worse, this sect claimed he was…God!

As the early church was advancing, its opponents were mounting counter measures. The apostles were arrested and beaten but that was not enough to stop the fire from spreading. Being in Jerusalem, the Jewish epicenter of the world, those loyal to the Jewish faith could not take this lying down. When a rising leader in the church, Stephen, began to speak boldly for Jesus, he was met with the starkest opposition. While on trial in front of the Jewish ruling council, Stephen made a speech for the ages. He basically criticized the people in the room and their parentage for their constant unwillingness to listen to the God they claimed to follow. You know how you would feel if someone talked about your momma.

The crowd was so riled that they picked up stones and pelted him, resulting in his death. This is significant to our current discussion because of what Luke records at the end of this account:

And Saul approved of their killing him. (Acts 8:1a)

It did not take long for approval to turn into participation; one might say that the condoning of an activity is participation by implication. Luke continues:

> *On that day a great persecution broke out against the church in Jerusalem, and all except the apostles were scattered throughout Judea and Samaria. ²Godly men buried Stephen and mourned deeply for him. ³But Saul began to destroy the church. Going from house to house, he dragged off both men and women and put them in prison.* (Acts 8:1b-3)

Saul was not a happy camper when it came to Christians. He was full of hatred and determined to leave no stone unturned (or on the ground) as he sought to "destroy the church." For him, being a man or woman was irrelevant; if you claimed to be a follower of Jesus, you had to pay the price, no matter who you were. Indeed, the words of his letter to Galatian churches ring true:

> *¹³For you have heard of my previous way of life in Judaism, how intensely I persecuted the church of God and tried to destroy it. ¹⁴I was advancing in Judaism beyond many of my own age among my people and was extremely zealous for the traditions of my fathers.* (Galatians 1:13-14)

Saul's story takes a sharp turn as his campaign takes him to Damascus. Having received written permission from the high priest to arrest any Jesus followers and bring them to Jerusalem, he encounters Jesus himself. This is like the classic case of a kid being bullied in school, only for his big brother to show up on the scene; this is typically bad news for the bully. The likely result is that the bully never messes with the little brother again.

Jesus, the big brother in God's family (Romans 8:29), confronted Saul. The encounter is as follows:

> [4]*He fell to the ground and heard a voice say to him, "Saul, Saul, why do you persecute me?"* [5]*"Who are you, Lord?" Saul asked. "I am Jesus, whom you are persecuting," he replied.* [6]*"Now get up and go into the city, and you will be told what you must do."* (Acts 9:4-6)

Saul did not mess with Jesus' little brother after this.

What did happen, though, was truly remarkable. Having traveled to Damascus to hunt Christians, he ends up helping them!

> *Saul spent several days with the disciples in Damascus.* [20]*At once he began to preach in the synagogues that Jesus is the Son of God.* [21]*All those who heard him were astonished and asked, "Isn't he the man who raised havoc in Jerusalem among those who call on this name? And hasn't he come here to take them as prisoners to the chief priests?"* [22]*Yet Saul grew more and more powerful and baffled the Jews living in Damascus by proving that Jesus is the Messiah.* (Acts 9:19b-22)

Those loyal Jews who heard him speaking in the synagogues were in disbelief. Wasn't this the guy they had heard was going to take down the Nazarenes for good? Is he now saying this heretic, Jesus, is actually the Messiah and Son of God? No one, though, was more incredulous than the disciples of Jesus. Nobody wanted to have anything to do with Saul because of how sorely they had been beaten up by him. You know it's bad when the guy who baptizes you is having reservations (Acts 9:10-19).

While a little rocky at first, Saul was eventually accepted into the Christian fellowship; of course, he was later acknowledged as an apostle. Aptly known as the Apostle to the Gentiles, he traveled the world preaching the gospel message. Eventually, his gospel journey would culminate in a final visit to Rome.[11]

Before his arrival, and now known to everyone as *Paul*, he writes to Christians who lived in Rome. With his days as a persecutor of the church in the past, he makes a claim that would be earth-shattering to anyone nearly as devoted to the Jewish faith as he once was:

> [1]*I speak the truth in Christ—I am not lying, my conscience confirms it through the Holy Spirit—* [2]*I have great sorrow and unceasing anguish in my heart.* [3]*For I could wish that I myself were cursed and cut off from Christ for the sake of my people, those of my own race,* [4]*the people of Israel. Theirs is the adoption to sonship; theirs the divine glory, the covenants, the receiving of the law, the temple worship and the promises.* [5]*Theirs are the patriarchs, and from them is traced the human ancestry of the Messiah, who is God over all, forever praised! Amen.*
> (Romans 9:1-5)

The Messiah, Jesus, is not only related to every descendant of Abraham but he is also *God over all*. From his encounter while en route to Damascus until his dying breath, Paul lived his life in light of this profession; history records his service as perhaps the greatest to the cause of Christ. The Jesus whom he persecuted was all along the God he had pledged his life to serve.

---

11   Hart, D. B. (2015). *The story of Christianity: A history of 2,000 years of the Christian faith*. New York, NY: Quercus.

PART 2–

ALL MAN

When interacting with Jesus, people were largely unaware that they were interacting with God. They did, however, know they were addressing a man.

We may not be able to now but there was a time when Jesus could be seen and touched – we will, though, see him one day (1 John 3:2)! People interacted with him just like we do our family, friends and co-workers on a daily basis. In fact, if God were to restore humanity to right relationship with himself, he would have to do so as a man.

NEW AND IMPROVED

According to the Scriptures, the human race started with one man: Adam (Genesis 2:7). It was God's intent for Adam to be his representative to all creation, expanding God's dominion by producing godly offspring and subduing the earth in increasing measure; he would, of course, need a helper for this task: Eve. The responsibility given to them would be passed down to each human being who would come to exist. Like in a poorly played game of telephone, though, the message did not get very far down the line.

While Adam and Eve remained the sole representatives of God on earth, they encountered their first adversary: Satan. Though opposing God is certainly not a good decision, he is crafty in the way he goes about it. Having failed in his initial rebellion in heaven (Luke 10:18), Satan had now set his sights on God's chief creation. He didn't come at them with knives, swords or even guns but instead a lie. He convinced Eve, who then convinced Adam, that they should rule the earth independently of God. They rebelled against God, bringing upon themselves and all of us the most severe of consequences. Instead of passing on the blessing of obedience, Adam and Eve subjected humanity to sin and death.

Not at all satisfied with leaving man in this condition, God had resolved to provide a solution – insert Jesus. He knew this was a problem needing divine intervention, one that would need to be addressed at its core. Since the problem started with a man, it would also have to be ended by a man. Humanity needed someone to take the fall for what Adam had done, simultaneously winning the battle with sin and death once-and-for-all. Through this sacrificial victory, all would be able to experience the life God had desired for them to live. Paul writes concerning this:

> *For if, by the trespass of the one man, death reigned through that one man, how much more will those who receive God's abundant provision of grace and of the gift of righteousness reign in life through the one man, Jesus Christ!* (Romans 5:17)

God had always intended for his blessing to come through one man. At the onset of creation, this man was Adam. After he sinned, God needed another man. Over the course of biblical history, different men had risen to prominence who presented themselves as candidates for this position:

- Noah – God restarted humanity with his family after the flood, having built an ark to preserve their lives as well as two of every kind of animal.

- Abraham – God promised all people would be blessed through him; his family became God's chosen people.

- Moses – God called him to rescue his people from Egypt, doing miraculous signs through him.

- Joshua – God called him to lead his people to take possesion of the land promised to them.

- David – God chose him to be king of Israel, promising to establish his royal line forever.

- Solomon – God gave him unparalleled wisdom and wealth as he led the nation of Israel to unprecedented prosperity.

- Elijah – God called him to prophesy during one of Israel's steepest periods of spiritual decline, also doing miraculous signs through him; he did not experience death but was taken up to heaven.

- John the Baptist – God called him to lead Israel to spiritual renewal, after hundreds of years of prophetic silence.

While all of these men are great, they all have one issue: sin. Just as in the case of Adam, sin disqualifies one from occupying this seat. In this short list, there are some seemingly near misses – if I didn't know better, I would have voted for Abraham – but sin creates a chasm that is too vast for any of us to cross. Since Jesus was able to win the battle with sin, he earned the right to grant the blessing of grace and righteousness to those who would receive it. What Jesus did trumped what Adam had done; those who had died by Adam's trespass were able to live because of Christ's obedience. Jesus is the new Adam.

God did not go about the last Adam in the same way he did the first. Breathing into the dust of the ground was good but something better would be required if Adam 2.0 would accomplish God's divine ends. This time, things needed to be different, and God ensured this would be the case. Paul, again, gives some commentary on the matter:

> [45]*So it is written: "The first man Adam became a living being;" the last Adam, a life-giving spirit.* [46]*The spiritual did not come first, but the natural, and after that the spiritual.* [47]*The first man was of the dust of the earth; the second man is of heaven.* [48]*As*

was the earthly man, so are those who are of the earth; and as is the heavenly man, so also are those who are of heaven. [49]And just as we have borne the image of the earthly man, so shall we bear the image of the heavenly man. (1 Corinthians 15:45-49)

Jesus, the last Adam, did not come from the earth but from heaven. He was, make no mistake about it, human in every respect. The difference is Jesus was not merely natural but spiritual. If any of us are to have a fighting chance against sin, we need a spiritual life. We are granted life in the Spirit when we believe in Jesus.

Not only does Paul highlight Jesus' superiority over Adam but also God's intention in sending the Son. He is God's new representative and we will one day bear the image of the one from heaven. While Paul, here, speaks of the fulfillment of this reality, John speaks of the day-to-day implications of it: "Whoever claims to live in him must live as Jesus did" (1 John 2:6).

Simply stated, each of us is called to be like Jesus.

JUST LIKE US

Being like Jesus can be an intimidating notion. When we read of all of his feats, and his lack of flaws and failures, it has the potential to lead us to a mild depression. This can also be the case when we compare ourselves to other flawed people.

As a pastor I am responsible for being a moral and spiritual example for people. This can sometimes be confused with being a superhero, which I certainly am not. In a counseling session I was having with a married couple, the husband reluctantly conveyed he had been having difficulty in his spiritual walk; things like reading the Bible and praying were simply not happening. It was clear that he felt somewhat undone having said that to me. There, though, was a shift in his demeanor as our conversation progressed. It went from discouragement and shame to courage and confidence.

What was it that caused this change?

When I began to tell him how much I could actually relate to him, our conversation took on a different tone. I was not perceived as someone on a pedestal talking down to him but an empathizer who wanted to help. Granted, I was reading my Bible and praying regularly at the time of our talk, but it didn't mean the sentiment was something foreign. Likewise, Jesus goes out of his way to let us know he can empathize with us. Here is what the writer of Hebrews says:

> [14]*Therefore, since we have a great high priest who has ascended into heaven, Jesus the Son of God, let us hold firmly to the faith we profess.* [15]*For we do not have a high priest who is unable to empathize with our weaknesses, but we have one who has been tempted in every way, just as we are—yet he did not sin.* [16]*Let us then approach God's throne of grace with confidence, so that we may receive mercy and find grace to help us in our time of need.* (Hebrews 4:14-16)

Jesus may not know what it is like to sin, but he does know what it is like to struggle. He has had a bad day. He has been treated unfairly. He has had family drama. To him, the struggle is real.

Even though Jesus is the perfect example to which we should aspire, he is merciful and gracious when we find it difficult to emulate him. Why? He has been tempted in every way. When we feel the pressures of life bearing down on us, we are able to look to Jesus for our cues and also our comfort. He wants to help us, as the fullest expression of life is found is his example.

OUR SAVIOR

Jesus Christ is not just an amazing man but also our Savior.

The writers of Scripture convey the need for humanity to be saved, and God's willingness to meet this need. There are many people, perhaps even yourself, who have found this to be true. They have put their hope and trust in the God who is able to rescue them, having identified this God as Jesus. Maybe, though, you are reading this and have not made the same decision. You may be asking, "Why do I *need* to be saved?"

The word "need" can be quite relative. Our needs are embedded in our natural desires but this is sometimes confused for what we simply *want*. For instance, nobody really needs a mansion, even though it would certainly be nice to own one. On the contrary, we all have a desire for lodging, which is reflexive of our common need for shelter. We may say we need something but can in fact go without it just fine.

Is this the case with Jesus as well? While I would say there are many reasons why we should want him, being Savior does speak to our common need for him. Why else would he identify himself in this way?

When some think of religion, factoring Jesus into this equation, they compare it to being sold a car. Each salesman, on each car lot, is pulling out all the stops to get our money in exchange for what we hope is a quality vehicle, which we sometimes cannot even afford. They highlight every feature in order to pique our interest, and even entice us with incentives in order to seal the deal. Thinking back, this is how I ended up with a Mercedes Benz as my first car, instead of the Toyota Corolla I intended to buy. Credit to the salesman who pulled that one off!

Jesus, though, is not trying to sell anything. He does not need anything from us but recognizes we need everything from him. In looking at the world around us, we see things that are beautiful and that bring us joy but also things that are tragic and cause for despair. What do we make of people killing each other out of sheer hatred, whether in America or other parts of the world? What of gang violence? Addiction? Sex trafficking? Money, education and reform are certainly things that can help but we know these societal ills are too difficult for those things to cure in their entirety. Ultimately, we all find ourselves in the same spiritual captivity as ancient Israel, to whom God said:

I, even I, am the Lord, and apart from me there is no savior.
(Isaiah 43:11)

Indeed, Jesus is not a car salesman who is trying to get us to buy from him instead of some other religion; again, apart from him there is no savior. He is, instead, the head of state that is able to grant pardon to anyone held captive in the prison of sin. No doubt, each of us has been in this prison, simply by virtue of being born; this is confirmed by our inability to always do what is right.

Have you ever told a lie, even the slightest fib?

You're a prisoner.

Have you ever taken something that belonged to someone else without asking?

Prisoner.

Have you ever wished ill upon some else?

Prisoner.

While we can probably make a list of moral failures longer than this book, it does not really matter what we have done. You're familiar with the classic portrayal of inmates where one asks the question, "What are you in for?" Regardless of how the answers vary, the point is that each prisoner is *in*! In the U.S. criminal justice system, sentences are made in keeping with the severity of the offense. One person may receive five years, while another may be in for life. The justice of God, however, demands the same sentence for each transgression: "For the wages of sin is death" (Romans 6:23a).

Thanks be to God for Jesus Christ who is willing to amend this sentence! As quick as he is to convey the consequences of sin, he also espouses his desire for us to be released from our prison to live forever with him: "but the gift of God is eternal life in Christ Jesus our Lord" (Romans 6:23b). His atoning death and triumphant resurrection give him the authority to grant the gift of pardon and a new life to anyone who comes to him.

Maybe you feel your crimes are too heinous to be forgiven. Perhaps you are even carrying guilt from a decision you made years ago? I assure you, if you come to Jesus, there is nothing he will not forgive. I was once in this prison, awaiting the death penalty, but I asked Jesus to free me. And guess what? He did! As Jesus says, "So if the Son sets you free, you are truly free" (John 8:36 NLT).

If you are reading this and have not made the decision to make Jesus your Lord and Savior, I want to encourage you to do so. All of us need saving, and Jesus is the only one who can meet this need. It is a simple exchange really; if you ask Jesus for forgiveness, he will forgive you and give you new, eternal, life. In an effort to help you, I have given you some words you can use as you talk to him:

> *Jesus, I thank you for being willing to meet my greatest need, which is my need for a savior. I recognize that you are this savior, because you alone are God. Though I am guilty, you remove my guilt by your atoning death. Though I was bound for death, through your resurrection, I am able to receive life. I make the decision, today, to receive what you have done for me. No longer will I live as a prisoner of sin, but as a servant of my Lord and my God. Amen.*

My sincere prayer is that every person reading this has made Jesus their savior, receiving forgiveness for sins and experiencing the life he is so desirous to give. This is the best life we could ever live, and the greatest part about it is that it does not end! It is truly amazing that Jesus is the God who is able to save. When we begin this saving relationship, our commitment is to follow him wherever he should lead. The reality of our following him, though, is deeply entrenched in him becoming a man.

This brings us back to Paul's opening words to the Philippians. Yes, he told of how God became a man. Even still, he describes how he set aside his divine rights and privileges, served and, ultimately, died for us. His point, though, is clearly seen in the words leading into this description of Jesus: "In your relationships with one another, *have the same mindset as Christ Jesus*" (emphasis added). Paul intended for Christ's example to affect the way his audience related to the people around them. As we continue on our journey of discovering more of his amazing life, my heart is for each of us to be empowered to emulate him in every way.

SECTION ONE:

"AN AMAZING SON" –
JESUS THE SON OF MARY AND JOSEPH

Luke 2:4-5

> [4]*So Joseph also went up from the town of Nazareth in Galilee*
> *to Judea, to Bethlehem the town of David, because he belonged*
> *to the house and line of David.* [5]*He went there to register with*
> *Mary, who was pledged to be married to him and was expect-*
> *ing a child.*

Life, much like a race, has a starting line.

As we each navigate our way through life, it will take shape uniquely, based on our differing environments. Each of us, though, has shared at least one experience: birth.

How amazing is it that Jesus himself would also participate in this universal phenomenon? Though he is the Son of God, he did not exempt himself from becoming the son of man, being born to both Mary and Joseph. Jesus becoming "fully human" meant he would have parents, just like the rest of us.

To be sure, not everyone's starting line is the same. Things such as economic status, ethnicity, nationality or locale are often perceived as advantages or disadvantages, depending on the view. Jesus shows us that when we can best manage our beginning – regardless of how we start – it will help us finish strong. We will then explore how Jesus managed the ups and downs of his beginnings and how we can do likewise.

CHAPTER 1:

"HAPPY BIRTHDAY"

Jesus' welcoming into the world was humble, yet eventful.

His parents were not well to do or people of repute (at least not back then) but were quite ordinary. Joseph was a carpenter by trade (Matthew 13:55) and Mary likely planned on a life as a homemaker. They probably had dreams of how their future together would unfold asking, "Will we live in this small town of Nazareth forever?" or "How many children will we have?" We are not certain of how old they were when they tied the knot but we do know Mary was a virgin upon being betrothed to Joseph. As devout Jews, they aspired to be the kind of parents who raised their children with impeccable morals. While this may have been the case Mary was found pregnant during their engagement, even though Joseph had not laid a finger on her.

I told you it was eventful.

Stories of Jesus' birth are fabled enough for us all to know Mary had not stepped out on Joseph. She was sincerely devoted to him and, most importantly, to God. Besides, in her day, there were legal deterrents to being found pregnant with someone's child other than your husband; let's just say that it involved rocks (Deuteronomy 22:20-24). No, this was not a case of immorality but of immaculate conception as she became pregnant by the

Holy Spirit. For the next nine months Mary would carry the most amazing child. Then the time came for him to finally be born.

Because of a Roman-issued census (Luke 2:1), Joseph and Mary traveled from their town of Nazareth to Bethlehem at least a three-day journey[12]; Joseph was required to register there due to his lineage. Road trips are not my favorite thing in the world but I would much rather drive a car than ride on a donkey, especially when accompanied by a woman with child. Rest stops, I'm sure, looked a lot differently in the first century.

You can imagine then the desperation of this couple to find somewhere to stay as soon as they reached Bethlehem. They had a hard time finding lodging, likely because of the influx of travelers. This meant they had to take what they could get, eventually settling for a stable. Not able to wait any longer, Mary gave birth to her firstborn son. Yes, it was in a manger that Jesus made his arrival into the world. Talk about humble beginnings.

Thinking of this incredible moment is very sobering to me. Now, being a father, Jesus' birth narrative feels much more real and less like the storybook version I grew up hearing. When the time came for Marshall to be born, my wife and I knew the hospital we would go to, the route we'd take to get there and were even familiar with the facility. Regardless of any jitters of being new parents, we knew our baby would be born in one of the best hospitals in the United States, maybe even the world, with around-the-clock care.

Joseph and Mary, on the contrary, probably had assumed Jesus would be born in their hometown of Nazareth. Instead, they had to travel at least three days to Bethlehem with the possibility of their baby coming any day. Whatever plans they may have made were thrown out the window. I'm not sure if birth plans were a thing back then but to many making even the slightest of adjustments to these plans can be stressful.

It was, though, God's plan for Jesus' birth to unfold this way. You may ask, "How do you know this?" I'll give you a couple of reasons.

---

12   NIV84 (Zondervan) note on Luke 2:4

The prophet Micah foretold of the day the Messiah would make his debut:

> *But you, Bethlehem Ephrathah,*
>
> *though you are small among the clans of Judah,*
>
> *out of you will come for me*
>
> *one who will be ruler over Israel,*
>
> *whose origins are from of old,*
>
> *from ancient times.* (Micah 5:2)

It is clear from Matthew's retelling of King Herod's conversation with the priests and scribes that this passage was understood as a reference to the birth of the Messiah, which is Christ (Matthew 2:4-6). It is no coincidence then that Jesus was born in Bethlehem – it was planned.

I did promise you a second reason as well, which we find in the Proverbs:

> *The king's heart is a stream of water in the hand of the LORD;*
> *he turns it wherever he will.* (Proverbs 21:1 ESV)

It was the census issued by Caesar Augustus, Rome's reigning imperial power, which triggered the events leading to Jesus' birth in Bethlehem. What merely seemed a way to account for every inhabitant of the Roman Empire was really the result of a divine plan that had been in motion. God turned Augustus' heart in a direction that would end up benefitting the entire world, not just promote the grandeur of Rome.

Maybe Jesus' birth story is causing you to reflect on your own. Perhaps you were born into less than ideal circumstances? Maybe you were born as a result of them? I can relate to this.

My mother and father never married. Having been high school sweethearts, they had dreams of how their future together would look but did not make it to the altar. Instead, my parents actually broke up while my mother was pregnant with me; from what I'm told, my dad was not present when I was born. Eventually, though, they reunited. I even remember as a very young child a time when we all lived in the same house. This was until the fateful day when my father was sent to prison with two life sentences.

Being born in inner city Detroit came with its own challenges. Detroit has been a very distressed place. In fact, the city notoriously filed for bankruptcy in 2013, the largest American city to ever have done so.[13] While money may have been scarce, we never seemed to run out of tough times when I was growing up.

I can recall a particular season I did not really enjoy. We were renting a house on the west side of the city. It was not the nicest house but it was what we could afford; eventually, this stopped being the case. As a kid, there are lots of things you do not immediately realize. For me, I was unaware of just how dangerous our neighborhood was. One day this blissful ignorance came to a screeching halt.

When I was about nine, I was playing baseball with my cousin and best friend in my backyard. We'd done this plenty of times and had baseballs in my rear neighbor's yard to prove it; those baseballs are probably still there. It is hard to remember who was up to bat but what I do remember was surreal. The impact of my aluminum bat on the ball made a pretty loud sound but the sound I heard that day was infinitely louder. It was the sound of my ignorance fading. It was the sound of me coming to terms with my reality. It was the sound of a gunshot.

When I turned to run for the backdoor of my house, I saw a scene I will never forget. Several police officers were running for cover behind vehicles parked on the street – I don't know if I have seen a police officer run at all since that day, unless it was on TV. Yes, someone had just opened fire on the people who are called to protect and serve…and they were running for cover. With my mom struggling to unlock the door, I felt so vulnerable, so

---

13   Davey, M., & Walsh, M. (2013, July 18). Billions in Debt, Detroit tumbles into insolvency. Retrieved March 11, 2021, from https://www.nytimes.com/2013/07/19/us/detroit-files-for-bankruptcy.html

scared, so unsafe. I was so desperate to get inside that I ran around to the front door – this was probably the worst idea I have had in my entire life. Eventually, we did get inside safely. I was reeling in disbelief; we were taking cover during a police shootout. After the dust settled, we learned the police were busting a prominent drug operation. All this time, I had been living right across the street.

While you may be inclined to have sympathy for me, this is not the point of my sharing. Each of our experiences, while unique, is in some way "less than ideal." We cannot control the circumstances surrounding our birth – who, what, when, where, why or how. Maybe this had led to disappointment, heartache or even resentment? What can we glean from the earliest stage of Jesus' life to help us? My friends, it is this:

The circumstances of your birth do not determine the outcome of your life.

Yes, Jesus was born as a result of an unbelievable pregnancy story.

No, Jesus' parents were not rich and famous.

Yes, Jesus' people – the Jews – were under rule of Rome, so much so that his parents had to take a three-day trip for tax purposes preceding his birth.

No, Jesus was not born in a place any of us would likely choose.

In the end, these things did not put a cap on Jesus' life. On the contrary, they were all a part of God's unfolding plan for him and the world. God certainly *uses* the circumstances of each of our birth narratives but it is he alone who *determines* the outcome of our lives. He knows the plans he has for us, which is why the host of heaven can rejoice when the baby of an unwed mother is born in a manger (Luke 2:8-14); maybe this is also true for a baby born to an unwed mother in Detroit.

When looking at the plain facts of Jesus' early life, you would not suspect he would be a person of even remote significance. He, though, is not only the subject of this book but also many others, including the most famous book of all-time: The Bible. Could it be that God had the most important human being be born in the most obscure circumstances to teach us this lesson?

Though he was a king, he was not born in a palace. He was a priest and a prophet but was not born in the religious epicenter of Jerusalem. Instead, he identified with the nearby shepherds, not the most heralded of occupations in his day. This ended up marking Jesus' life, as he would later identify himself as "the Good Shepherd" (John 10:11).

Maybe you have a disability from birth? Perhaps you were born in a difficult environment? It could have even been hard growing up with your unique parenting dynamics. I assure you, not only has God accounted for those things but wants to use them. He can use disability to testify to the strength that he gives; a difficult environment to forge our character and inform our calling; unique parenting dynamics to point people to their Father in heaven.

While I did not choose any of the circumstances I was born into, I am the person I am today because of them. I'm not a drug dealer, though I lived across the street from one. I do not have children apart from marriage, even though this was the case with my own parents. I am not frequently moving from place to place because of financial instability, although I experienced this growing up. I am a pastor, a proud husband and father, and a homeowner, by God's grace. God used each facet of my journey like a skilled sewing artist, intricately weaving his unique design for my life.

This is the case with each of us, including his own Son.

CHAPTER 2:

"HOME ALONE"

Jesus, just like the rest of us, would eventually grow up.

He experienced the transition from newborn to infant, infant to toddler and toddler to adolescent. We know very little about this time in his life, so we are left simply to question and speculate.

Was he a frequent crier? How terrible were his twos? Did he get straight A's? Perfect attendance? I cannot imagine he was ever on punishment.

While he may have never gotten into trouble, he did share a common experience with my favorite childhood purveyor of mischief: Kevin McCallister (aka Macaulay Culkin). The *Home Alone* movies, in particular the second installment, are among my favorite to watch. This is such a known fact that my wife gifted me a DVD set of the first two films, one year for Christmas. Watching them at Christmastime has become somewhat of a Ballenger family tradition.

Just by reading the title you can probably guess what happens to eight-year old Kevin even if you have not seen the movie: he is left at home… alone. After his parents unwittingly leave him behind in a mad dash for their flight to France, he ends up using a series of booby-traps to thwart the plot of two burglars, who had planned on the McCallisters being out-of-town for the holidays. However, they come back home to find Kevin safe and sound. This is, of course, until the following year when they are separated from Kevin in another scurry to the airport; if it's any consolation, they had multiple children.

Maybe they should have employed the buddy system?

This, it seems, is not just an issue for the modern traveler but also those traveling in the first century. Mary and Joseph, while heading back to Nazareth from Jerusalem after the Passover, actually misplaced their now twelve-year-old son. Fortunately for them, Jesus knew how to handle himself. Here is how Luke tells the story:

> *43After the festival was over, while his parents were returning home, the boy Jesus stayed behind in Jerusalem, but they were unaware of it. 44Thinking he was in their company, they traveled on for a day. Then they began looking for him among their relatives and friends. 45When they did not find him, they went back to Jerusalem to look for him. 46After three days they found him in the temple courts, sitting among the teachers, listening to them and asking them questions. 47Everyone who heard him was amazed at his understanding and his answers. 48When his parents saw him, they were astonished. His mother said to him, "Son, why have you treated us like this? Your father and I have been anxiously searching for you."* (Luke 2:43-48)

Though Kevin's separation from his family was accidental this did not seem to be the case with Jesus, at least on his part.

Having reached an age of maturity as a Jewish male, this trip to Jerusalem was likely much different for him. While parents were instructed to tell their children about the meaning of Passover (Exodus 12:26-27), there came a point in time when the faith of the father became the faith of the son. Perhaps on this visit to the Holy City, the festival had new meaning? Maybe, also, the temple had a new sense of grandeur? Clearly, though, Jesus' relationship with the God of his father had become personal.

Mary and Joseph had forgotten their son, not realizing it until after a day's worth of travel. It took them at least another two days before they finally located him. Jesus, however, was not phased. He was not rattled. In fact, sitting amongst the teachers of the law, it was they who were *amazed* at this remarkable twelve-year-old, who seemed very comfortable even though unsupervised in the temple.

Added to the teachers' amazement was the astonishment of Jesus' parents when they finally found him. He'd been missing for at least three days but was not *lost in Jerusalem*; he might have even been right where they left him. Mary and Joseph, undoubtedly overwhelmed with emotion, ask him why he had treated them this way. They had been anxiously searching for him, perhaps even thinking the worst. All the while, he was just sitting in the temple, almost as if they had simply dropped him off at school.

While Jesus is the Son of God, I would not recommend his reply to his parents' question: "Why were you searching for me?" (Luke 2:49a). I doubt any of our parents would take this answer well if we had gone missing for 72 hours. In our day, even the police would be involved at this point. I would imagine a night in jail could be a consequence for this type of reaction.

What he says next, though, was most puzzling to Mary and Joseph:

> *"Didn't you know I had to be in my Father's house?"* [50]*But they did not understand what he was saying to them.* (Luke 2:49b-50)

They may not have understood but Jesus was not necessarily concerned about this. Sure, they were his parents well enough, but he had come to the realization of his divine parentage. In the absence of Mary and Joseph, Jesus was assured of his relationship with his Heavenly Father, finding refuge in his house; this is, in fact, the reason he went missing in the first place.

This scene in Jesus' life paints us a picture. We all have earthly parents but also a Heavenly Father. Yes, Jesus is in closest relationship with the Father (John 1:18). That he "grew in wisdom and stature, and in favor with God and man" (Luke 2:52), however, means he cultivated his relationship with his God-dad as well as his mom and dad. Sometimes, though, our relationship with the Father will lead us to do things that our "parents just don't understand."[14]

Jesus' relationship with his heavenly Father did not come at the expense of the one with his earthly parents. Even after Mary and Joseph left him, "he went down to Nazareth with them and was obedient to them" (2:51). As he grew in his relationship with the Father, though, it is clear he gained a greater understanding of his own identity. How could the sinless Son of God submit himself to parents who were going to make mistakes? Disappoint him? Give him wrong advice?

Here's how we should process the example of our Lord:

Having a healthy relationship with our Heavenly Father allows us to have healthy expectations of our earthly parents.

Each of us, fundamentally, is flawed, and our parents are no exception to this. Even for those of us who had the best of parents, inevitably they commit some kind of blunder.

Maybe it was a missed game or a recital that was very important to you? Perhaps careless words were spoken to you after your mom and/or dad had a tough day at work?

Intimately knowing our Heavenly Father is what allows our hearts to remain tempered. Are we still liable to have our feelings hurt on occasion? Well, yes; I would even encourage talking about these things when they happen. In our Father, though, we find the same refuge Jesus did when he was without his parents in the temple for three days. There is always room for us in the Father's house.

As an adult, Jesus speaks of the similarity but also clear distinction between our earthly parents and Heavenly Father. He says:

---

14   "Parents Just Don't Understand." Harris, Smith, Townes (1988)

9 "Which of you, if your son asks for bread, will give him a stone? 10Or if he asks for a fish, will give him a snake? 11If you, then, though you are evil, know how to give good gifts to your children, how much more will your Father in heaven give good gifts to those who ask him! (Matthew 7:9-11)

While speaking on the topic of prayer, Jesus uses the parent-child relationship as a framework. He addresses the parents in the crowd with some rhetorical questions, knowing full well the answers are obvious. No parent would give their kid a stone or snake if they were hungry, not unless they wanted protective services to get involved. Parents know how to give good gifts to their children when they ask, and so does our Father in heaven. The difference lies in the evil inclination Jesus identifies within the human heart. Even the most noble and sincere efforts of parents will eventually result in failure of some kind. Though the gifts parents give may be *good*, they will never be *perfect*.

Jesus' brother James adds the following:

16Don't be deceived, my dear brothers and sisters. 17Every good and perfect gift is from above, coming down from the Father of the heavenly lights, who does not change like shifting shadows (James 1:16-17)

The Father is not the author of evil but the author of good. In fact, everything that is good and perfect comes from him. His unchanging nature means we have in him perfect consistency. He always says what he means and does what he says, and his word is true. Knowing this, knowing *him*, in the deepest places of our hearts allows him to parent us through the failings, inconsistencies and unfulfilled promises in this life – even if they are in our own home.

Can I give you a piece of advice?

Let your parents off the hook.

They are not perfect people but we've clearly established there is no such thing.

When Heidi and I were dating, we took a trip to Detroit for her to meet my family. I knew she was "the one," and wanted my loved ones to get used to seeing her pretty face. As we toured the place where I grew up, not only were many memories stirred but also emotions I had not experienced in years – the good, the bad and the ugly. On the last day of our trip, I had a time of prayer in my hotel room. While talking to my Father, I realized there was bitterness stored up in my heart toward my parents; I had felt abandoned, unprotected and unsupported. Whether it was justified or not, and bitterness is never justified, I knew I had to release them from things I was holding against them.

Did that make our relationships perfect? No. Is there still work to be done? Yes. Knowing the Father has given me a strength and solace that is truly not from this world. Where my parents may have lacked, my Father has been more than able to compensate.

Are you holding unto hurt from your childhood, or even your adulthood, from your mother or father? Look to *your* Father in heaven today. He will reveal his heart for you and give you a heart to forgive your parents when they fail, as we all do. Each us of ends up lacking something from our upbringing but the Father is able to provide what we need from the good and perfect gifts he has stored for us.

My encouragement to you is to not delay in talking with your mother and father. If there are things in your heart, it would be best for you to share them. Besides, what is more difficult than dealing with the mistakes of our parents is dealing with their loss.

CHAPTER 3:

"DEALING WITH LOSS"

Matthew and Luke's early accounts of Jesus' life make much mention of Joseph. Like some of us, Jesus' (earthly) dad may have been his hero. Based on Matthew's account alone, I would say he was nothing short of the word.

Joseph, when he found Mary to be pregnant during their engagement, having practiced celibacy, was simply going to break it off with her quietly; making this public would have had severe repercussions for her. An angel appeared to Joseph in a dream and consequently he agrees to take Mary and her unborn child into his home, and not consummate their marriage until he is born. Upon a visit from the three Magi, Joseph picks up and moves his family from Bethlehem to Egypt, having been warned in a dream of Herod's plot to kill Jesus. Then, after receiving the directive in yet another dream, he moves his family back to Nazareth (see Matthew 1 and 2).

From the snapshot the Scriptures give us of Joseph, it seems he was a dad's dad. He was a hard worker, as his professional reputation preceded him (Matthew 13:55). Not only did he do what was needed to provide for his family but also protected them, even if it meant moving to another country to do so. His compassion is displayed in how he had decided to handle Mary's pregnancy, prior to being visited by an angel with answers. Most importantly, he was the spiritual leader of his home. We know he was faithful to the law (Matthew 1:19) and maintained the customs of his day (Luke 2:22-24, 41-42) but also God spoke to him, which had a direct impact on his family.

As the gospel accounts progress, Joseph fades from the scene. The Scriptures do not explicitly address his absence but by implication, we can conclude his passing being the reason; Bible commentators take this view.[15] What was it like for Jesus to lose his father? What about when this happens to us?

While my heart goes out to everyone who has experienced loss of this kind, it is a heart of *sympathy*, not *empathy*. There are those in my life who have lost a parent. For some it was sudden. Others had time to say their goodbyes. While their stories differ, as does the relationship with their parents, it was equally difficult for each of these dear people.

Everyone can relate to loss of some kind. For me, losing my two grandfathers was really difficult. My mom's stepfather, Willie, was truly a hero. He married my grandmother, Earline, and took in her three daughters as if they were his very own. Today, the house he provided has been the setting for many family memories, also providing refuge when times were tough. Today, I am known as the guy who always has a peppermint in his pocket, but it is because he always carried them. Our family has never been the same since his loss.

My bond with my dad's dad, Johnny, deepened as I grew older. He had lost his wife when I was in middle school, so he lived all alone in the house where they raised their family. He was the closest connection I had to my father, after he went to prison, and he shared things about him no one else could. I always made it a point to visit him when I went back to Detroit, and I'm glad I did.

My wife and her family experienced the sudden loss of her older sister, Betsy. As a college senior, she was involved in a truck accident that took her life and that of four others. There is some part of us that feels burying

---

15   "Ellicott's Commentary for English Readers" and "Matthew Poole's Commentary" on John 19:26

a parent or grandparent is a natural course of life. A mom and dad burying their 22-year-old daughter though? I will never know the strength it took for my wife to address hundreds of mourners at the memorial.

Loss is a part of life, but it is seldom easy. There are so many things to think about upon the passing of a loved one. You are making funeral arrangements, notifying friends and comforting family, all the while trying to maintain your own sanity.

How did Jesus handle this? How did he navigate life after Joseph? How can we, after losing someone we love?

Our relationship with the Father is our comfort, refuge and hope when losing a loved one.

It's worth saying again that losing anyone is difficult, especially a parent. We do not have the benefit of seeing Jesus deal with his father's passing, but we can still glean some things to help us from his life. As Jesus' ministry was gaining more traction, he suddenly received news of the untimely death of another family member: John the Baptist.

We know Jesus and John were related from Luke's account of their prenatal lives. As the angel Gabriel is telling Mary about her amazing pregnancy, he makes reference to her "relative" Elizabeth, who was six months pregnant despite her old age (Luke 1:36). Their relation, though, we do not know exactly. Were they cousins? Was Elizabeth a great aunt? They were definitely close enough for Mary to stay with her for three months (Luke 1:56), probably until John was born. Either way, Mary and Elizabeth being related makes John and Jesus members of the same family.

The emphasis of the New Testament is really the ministry relationship of Jesus and John, not their family relationship. As such, we do not have many details concerning their interactions over the years. It is possible that they had playdates when they were little. They may have even gone to the same school. We do know, though, they thought very highly of each other.

John says of Jesus, "Look, the Lamb of God, who takes away the sin of the world! This is the one I meant when I said, 'A man who comes after me has surpassed me because he was before me.'" (John 1:29b-30). Not only did John say Jesus could solve the world's biggest problem but he acknowledged being outshone by the enduring light of the world.

Jesus, then, says the following concerning John: "Truly I tell you, among those born of women there has not risen anyone greater than John the Baptist" (Mark 11:11a). Can you pay a higher compliment to someone than this? I have never said anything this nice to anyone in my family.

When John's disciples deliver news of his death to Jesus, it naturally dealt him a blow. As Matthew records, "When Jesus heard what had happened, he withdrew by boat privately to a solitary place" (Matthew 14:13a).

While we need to be around others when we are grieving, we also need solitude. This allows us the opportunity to process emotions that can be easily buried under our busyness, the cares of life and convenient answers to the barrage of "How are you doing?" questions we may receive. For Jesus, his first inclination was to get in a boat alone and head to a solitary place. Upon reaching his destination, however, he quickly realized this would not be the case. The crowds had heard where he was going and decided to follow him on foot.

Though Jesus had every desire to be alone, there was a large crowd in front of him. By nature, I'm an introvert; this would have not been a good scene for me. So, what was his reaction? "He had compassion on them and healed their sick" (Matthew 14:14b). Jesus was hurting but seeing the crowds allowed him to recognize he was not the only one who was. The apostle Paul would speak to this in a letter to the Corinthians years later:

> [3]*Praise be to the God and Father of our Lord Jesus Christ, the Father of compassion and the God of all comfort, [4]who comforts us in all our troubles, so that we can comfort those*

in any trouble with the comfort we ourselves receive from God.
(2 Corinthians 1:3-4)

Could it be possible that experiencing the pain of losing John is actually what made Jesus as compassionate as he was in this moment? After all, according to Paul, our troubles allow us to experience God's comfort and, in turn, comfort others in their troubles. Our times of difficulty, then, qualify us to be the *comforted* and the *comforter*.

Jesus' plan of going to a "solitary place" was foiled, but he did travel there by boat "privately." We do not really know what took place while he was rowing his boat alone. This, however, seems like as good a time as any for Jesus to have wept for John. From the story of Lazarus, we know Jesus wept for the people he loved (John 11:35-36). His heart was moved by the loss of someone who had shared a part of his life. In the case of John the Baptist, it was an even harder loss, as his life was taken from him (Matthew 14:10). Growing up in the inner city, there were a lot of people whose lives were "taken." Gun violence was (and still is) a daily reality, with gang member and innocent bystander alike suffering its vicious consequences. My own family has shed tears because of this.

While teaching his disciples, Jesus actually speaks about loss. He says, "Blessed are those who mourn, for they will be comforted" (Matthew 5:4). If the expression "practice what you preach" means anything to Jesus, it makes sense that his time alone on the boat would be the place he initially mourned; this also echoes what we know of comfort's order – trouble, comforted, comforter. Not only did Jesus heal the sick among them but also performs perhaps his most famous miracle: the feeding of 5,000. This is the only miracle (besides rising from the dead) recorded by all four gospel writers, and I do not think it is a coincidence that Matthew records it on the heels of him finding out about his fallen relative. The Father wants to comfort us as we process the loss of our loved one but also use us to comfort others with the comfort we ourselves have received.

We do, though, have to actually go to the Father to receive this comfort.

It will not simply fall from the sky or be found at our bedside when we wake up in the morning; it is God's intent for us to find comfort *in him.* One of the great things about Jesus is that he is a man of the Scriptures. He often quoted the Psalms, which is a songbook full of theology and a wide range of emotions. I can imagine him thinking of a particular Psalm after hearing of John's passing:

> *God is our refuge and strength, an ever-present help in trouble.*
> (Psalm 46:1)

After his impromptu banquet he sent away the disciples, dismissed the crowds and "went up on a mountainside by himself to pray" (Matthew 14:23). When we lose someone, we do need to be alone sometimes, but what makes it most beneficial is when we go to God in prayer. It would appear this is the reason Jesus stepped into the boat in the first place. Why Jesus chose this particular location, I do not know. Whatever the reason, it was a place where he aspired to prayerfully take refuge in the Father.

There are so many things that can present themselves as a viable refuge when we are hurting from the loss of a loved one. Some people turn to alcohol or substances, while others may turn to food or media. Then there are those who have used sex to medicate the pain. After these things have been exhausted, we become keenly aware of their inability to provide adequate shelter. Choosing these things over God is like hiding under a cheap umbrella during a rainstorm, when we could just simply walk into a house – the Father's house. Only the Father is able to be our refuge in times of trouble. When finding refuge in him, we gain strength, one that is truly not our own. We also become conscious of his comforting presence all around us.

Knowing God is near should not only comfort us and give us strength but also hope. His comfort allows for the healing of our hearts and his strength gives our hearts resolve for the rest of our journey; acknowledging that the Father is with us carries us through it all. It was this knowledge of the Father's nearness which allowed Jesus, in the midst of mourning, to look up to heaven and *give thanks* in front of thousands of people for what seemed insufficient to meet the need. Not only did everyone eat but they were all "satisfied," with 12 baskets full of leftovers.

Brothers and sisters, though we may feel an overwhelming need for peace, joy or assurance after having experienced loss, we must believe the Father is able to turn our deficiency into an abundance. When our faith is most tried, it should be most exercised, and losing someone we love is definitely a time of testing. Yes, our struggles with loss are real but so also is God's all-sufficient grace, enduring mercy and steadfast love.

Maybe this discussion has brought feelings back to the surface you experienced after losing a loved one. It could even be possible that you just lost someone you love. Can I encourage you to do something counterintuitive?

Give thanks to God.

In doing so you not only go to him to find refuge and receive his comfort but also renew your hope in his goodness. This also helps to frame the time we had with our loved one as the gift from God that it truly was. Loss is always difficult, but it can become something sweet when we invite the Father into our grieving hearts. Everything is always better when the Father is involved.

CHAPTER 4:

"I GET NO RESPECT"

When you were a kid did you ever dream of how different things would be when you became an adult?

I know I did.

If you were anything like me, your dreams may have consisted of the following:

- No more bedtimes.

- No more eating my vegetables.

- No more being bossed around.

Though a nice thought, we all quickly realize how inaccurate these notions are when we grow older. Sleep is as precious as it has ever been, so now we race to our beds at night (and struggle to get out of them in the morning). Maintaining a healthy diet is not only more of a need but also more difficult, so we try to eat our veggies as much as we can. Not only are we still being told what to do but we identify our employers by the literal title "boss."

There is one possible change, though. Since we are all grown up, our parents should now respect us. With our own jobs, homes and personal lives, the dynamics of dependency have changed. We may not be equals with our parents but we are all adults. Shouldn't this mean being treated like one?

Jesus had come a long way since his parents took him to Jerusalem as a twelve-year-old. After Joseph's passing Jesus had taken on his trade of carpentry (Mark 6:3). At a certain point, he left the family business and devoted himself to full-time ministry, which is the Father's business.

Things seemed to be going well for Jesus. His teachings drew large crowds. People were getting healed. He even started to amass disciples who had pledged their lives to follow him. This, though, didn't seem to be enough to keep his mother and siblings from coming to take him home.

So much for being treated like an adult.

> *20Then Jesus entered a house, and again a crowd gathered, so that he and his disciples were not even able to eat. 21When his family heard about this, they went to take charge of him, for they said, "He is out of his mind."* (Mark 3:20-21)

Call me crazy but it seems like Jesus' family thought he was crazy. There are two things that come to mind upon realizing this:

1. If this can be said of Jesus, it can be said of anyone.

2. If being called "crazy" puts me in the same category as Jesus, I'm inclined to be less bothered by it.

The problem, though, lies in what his family did as a result of their thoughts of him: "they went to take charge of him." If saying that Jesus was "out of his mind" was even a remote lack of respect, going to interrupt his life and ministry went way over the line. However, this is a line they were willing to cross. In the event you thought they were bluffing, here is the proof:

> *31Then Jesus' mother and brothers arrived. Standing outside, they sent someone in to call him. 32A crowd was sitting around him, and they told him, "Your mother and brothers are outside looking for you."* (Mark 3:31-32)

Not only was Jesus with a crowd of people at the time but he was actually in the middle of an argument with some teachers of the law. Essentially, they had come from Jerusalem to discredit what he was doing, resorting to calling him demon-possessed. While in the midst of telling them why they were wrong, Jesus received the message of his family's arrival – talk about bad timing.

Each of us knows there are acceptable interruptions and those that are less tolerable. When I was a kid, sometimes my favorite cartoons would be halted by a test of the Emergency Broadcast System or to air a breaking news report – verdict: acceptable. Conversely, I have never been to the White House but I imagine it would be taboo to walk into the Oval Office to disrupt a meeting for a selfie with the president – verdict: unacceptable. This difference may be comical but we know having the important affairs of our lives disrupted is no laughing matter.

Like Jesus, our most important focus is the will of the Father. Indeed, everything is better when the Father is involved; that his will is "good, pleasing and perfect" (Romans 12:2) is proof positive of this. The Father's will, though, requires participation from each of his children. In this regard, Jesus' example is conveyed by the writer of Hebrews:

> [5]*Therefore, when Christ came into the world, he said:*
>
> *"Sacrifice and offering you did not desire,*
>
> *but a body you prepared for me;*
>
> [6]*with burnt offerings and sin offerings*
>
> *you were not pleased.*
>
> [7]*Then I said, 'Here I am—it is written about me in the scroll—*
>
> *I have come to do your will, my God.' "* (Hebrews 10:5-7)

The gospels, then, chronicle Jesus' participation in the Father's will. He preached repentance to sinners, taught them how to live in the kingdom of God, healed the sick and, ultimately, died for our sins; he of course also rose from the dead on the third day. Participation, however, only happens after an invitation. The Father's will is rooted in his "desire," and in order to see his will done on earth as it is in heaven (Matthew 6:10), he *calls* each of us to play a role. Fundamentally, the call is the same: advance the kingdom of God through the good news about Jesus. Each individual, however, does have things that are unique to the specific life they will live for God. One person may be a teacher, another an actor and someone else a police officer. Whatever the case, the Father deserves the same response from us that he received from Jesus: "I have come to do your will, my God."

If Jesus' life is any indication, there is work to be done once we embrace this call, which requires both our dedication and focus. Jesus says in John 9:4, "We must quickly carry out the tasks assigned us by the one who sent us. The night is coming, and then no one can work" (NLT). Needless to say, with a work this important, we would not want it to be disrupted. Surely, those we would expect to respect the urgency of this work would be our families; I think it is even reasonable to assume their support.

As Jesus is in the midst of fulfilling his calling, however, it is his family who interrupts him. They were not coming to bring a care package, nor was it a family emergency. Instead, they simply came to take him home. Not only did they withhold their support but also made known their protest of what he was doing – his own mother was the ringleader.

How did he process this? How do we?

Family is an important source of nurturing,
support and encouragement but these are not essential
in fulfilling God's call on our lives.

I am of the belief that our parents, and even families, are chosen by God. The seemingly endless list of genealogies in the Scriptures, namely that of Christ himself (see Matthew 1 and Luke 3), affirm the truth of this claim. What makes each of us who we are is the fact that two people's DNA came together to reproduce. For some of us this happened in the context of a loving marriage. Others may not have been as fortunate, perhaps having been born as a result of a casual encounter or even sexual abuse. While God does not condone those things, and is grieved when they happen, his plan accounts for these occurrences and he is able to ensure our arrival into history even if the landing is bumpy.

Did you know in Jesus' family history there were those born as a result of prostitution, forbidden marriage and adultery?

There are also those of us who have biological parents but were raised by someone else. This could have been another family member as in the case of Esther (Esther 2:7), or even an adopted family. God has a plan for each of us and, for some of us, it includes having people who love us brought into our lives to fill the role vacated by our birth mother and/or father. Even in the case of Jesus, Joseph was his dad but not biologically. He loved and protected Jesus as if he was born of his own seed.

While our parents may have been predetermined, we already know there are things we will inherently lack after having been raised by them. Even for those of us who had great parents, no one is perfect; at some point, there will be a deficiency. If the call of God was contingent upon what is inherently imperfect, who could ever fulfill it?

My friends, the call of God is not contingent upon what our families are able to offer us but on what God *desires* to do through us. When God wants to get something done, he will literally move heaven and earth to accomplish it. Helping us to overcome any obstacles on the home front is just the tip of the iceberg.

Sometimes, our families may struggle with God's calling upon our lives because it was unexpected, in certain cases more so to us than them. My pastor, Al Toledo, is one such example.

Al Toledo grew up in Brooklyn, NY. His parents came as immigrants from Cuba and did not raise him in the Christian faith but provided a loving home and a moral compass for him and his siblings. Very early on he discovered he had a talent for baseball. For years, he not only gave himself to the sport but developed into a promising professional prospect. Eventually, he was drafted by the Chicago White Sox. It seemed his life was all set.

At the age of 17, Jesus Christ came into Al's life. That this happened on a baseball field is both ironic and symbolic, as God would require his baseball career of him, instead calling him into the ministry. This was by no means an expedited journey but was one marked by loss, heartbreak and many questions. What added to the difficulty of this season of life was the protest of loved ones to his newfound path. Baseball was *all* he knew and *all* they knew. There were no other alternatives, and certainly not the ministry.

Despite their protest, he persevered.

As he aspired to grow in his newfound walk with the Lord, God continued to show himself faithful. He met his wife, Chrissy, at The Brooklyn Tabernacle, which was a significant training ground for him. His journey brought him to Omaha, NE, to serve a growing church in his first lead pastor role. He planted Chicago Tabernacle in 2002, the church where I met my wife and started my journey of pastoral ministry.

I, for one, am glad he persevered.

The same can certainly be said of our Lord and Savior. Though it seems Jesus' call was not nurtured, supported or encouraged by his family, he had the resolve to fulfill the Father's will. There were some lonely days. There were some difficult days. Despite it all he was able to endure because of the "joy set before him" (Hebrew 12:2), the joy of pleasing the Father.

At the core of our fulfillment of God's calling is a desire to please him. This is a desire that must be first in priority, amidst the opinions and demands of family. Because these opinions and demands are subject to change, them being the basis of how we live our lives for God is not only unwise but, ultimately, unproductive. While there is often good counsel offered to us by our families, parents in particular, there can very well be times when we have to stand on our own to make a decision in keeping with our calling.

So, what then? Does God just leave us to fend for the fulfillment of this call by ourselves?

Of course not.

We see in Jesus' response to the message from his family just how faithful God is when we pursue his purposes:

> [33] *"Who are my mother and my brothers?" he asked.* [34]*Then he looked at those seated in a circle around him and said, "Here are my mother and my brothers!* [35]*Whoever does God's will is my brother and sister and mother."* (Mark 3:33-35)

Jesus was not alone.

Though his mother and siblings may not have been on board with his ministry, there were those rallied around him who were also committed to God's will. It is clear that the Father sent these individuals into Jesus' life based on what he says in John 6:44: "No one can come to me unless the Father who sent me draws them." Even when we are not able to rely on our families, God sends brothers, sisters and mothers to nurture, support and encourage our calling. Fundamentally, this happens in the church. Specifically, there are individuals who are hand-picked to help us on our journey.

As you are reading this, I am sure you are reflecting on your journey thus far. Perhaps you have taken note of those who have been there for you and pushed you towards the call of God for your life. This nurturing, support and encouragement may not come from the people from whom you most desire it but God does provide it through others. What matters most, though, is for the Father's will to be realized, and it is the joy of pleasing him that motivates us to preserve. At the end of the day, this will not only benefit our own families but also the families of others.

I have a wife and a son to prove it.

CHAPTER 5:

"WHOSE SON AM I ANYWAY?"

Have you ever experienced the feeling of something being out-of-place? You know, when you observe a particular scene and conclude that something does not quite fit?

This happened to be the case on one occasion when my wife and I were driving together. While maybe not as intense as New York, Los Angeles or Atlanta, Chicago traffic can be quite a drag, especially at rush hour. As we were taking turns with the other drivers waiting at a particular stop light, we noticed something along the sidewalk. There was a man, as buff as Arnold Schwarzenegger and whose face was as stoic as a poker player, taking a walk in athletic gear. While this is not necessarily headline material, what made it noteworthy was that he was pushing a stroller with a smiling baby. The drivers around us also got a kick out of this.

Perhaps there was a time when you felt out-of-place? As youngsters, it seems we are constantly trying to find where we belong. This typically amounts to a roulette of extracurricular activities, attending any and every available social gathering and finding the appropriate table to sit in the school lunchroom. In these instances, and in general, I find that the reason we feel like we do not belong is typically because someone goes out of their way to tell us.

Jesus can relate to this sentiment.

Though people acknowledged the wisdom in his teaching as well as his special abilities, there were some who had difficulty giving him the stature of the priests, scribes or prophets. The reason: his family of origin.

> [54]*Coming to his hometown, he began teaching the people in their synagogue, and they were amazed. "Where did this man get this wisdom and these miraculous powers?" they asked.* [55]*"Isn't this the carpenter's son? Isn't his mother's name Mary, and aren't his brothers James, Joseph, Simon and Judas?* [56]*Aren't all his sisters with us? Where then did this man get all these things?"* [57]*And they took offense at him. But Jesus said to them, "A prophet is not without honor except in his own town and in his own home."* (Matthew 13:54-57)

Jesus was certainly a priest, in the sense that he came to dispense the Father's mercy, brining healing and forgiveness of sins. His teaching was more authoritative than any scribe, especially since the Scriptures were written about him (John 5:39). Certainly, Jesus was a prophet, as he proclaimed the heart and truth of God concerning the present and future realities of God's kingdom. Yes, he was very much aware of his calling, even identifying himself as a prophet in the above excerpt from Matthew. He would need to be certain of his kingdom vocation, since there was no basis for it in his immediate family.

The people in his town were not bashful in making this known.

While John the Baptist, for example, had a dad who served at the temple as a priest, Jesus was merely the son of a carpenter. It follows then that the religious establishment of the day had a measure of regard for John that they did not for Jesus. In fact, when Jesus' authority was questioned by the priests and elders in Jerusalem, he directed them to John's ministry as a means of reaching their own conclusion (Matthew 21:23-27). It didn't matter that Jesus' father was not "one of them," what mattered was that he was called.

Like Jesus, we may be called to lives much different than what we have seen or experienced growing up. Traditionally, we equate this with people whose upbringing was marked by adversity and have achieved success as adults, such as Tyler Perry and Oprah Winfrey. Sometimes, though, this different kind of living is not apparently an improvement. There are those whose families come from wealth, for instance, but who decided on pursuits leading them away from a life of opulence. Saint Claire of Assisi is one such example.[16]

Yes, our family relation and accompanying experiences contribute to our unique makeup as people. Our parents, especially, help shape our perceptions and preferences. However, being a part of a certain family does not fix the trajectory of the rest of our lives. We may receive our name from our parents but even this can be changed later in life. (In my estimation, the name change award goes to "Metta World Peace."[17]) What we learn from Jesus' ministry pursuits, as well as name changes, is this:

Our family associations do not determine our identity.

Validation is something we all have sought over the course of our lives. In keeping with our previous discussion, we can often look to those closest to us to affirm us. Additionally, most of us are willing to work ourselves to death in an effort to amass accolades we hope will convey our value to others. In many cases, though, who we are related to is what really matters, to others and ourselves.

I do not think it is wrong to take pride in our families of origin; I certainly would not recommend being ashamed. What I would say, however, is to not put too much stock into this. It is great to come from a family of doctors or lawyers. Embracing those family trends as personal identity,

---

16   Saint Clare of Assisi. (2020, October 06). Retrieved April 8, 2020, from https://www.biography.com/religious-figure/saint-clare-of-assisi

17   Deb, S. (2019, May 29). A reinvented metta world peace says he's finally at peace with the world. Retrieved April 8, 2020, from https://www.nytimes.com/2019/05/28/sports/metta-world-peace.html

nevertheless, could cause one to acquiesce to those particular paths when God may have something different. Conversely, coming from a family where there was substance abuse and instability by no way means this is all that is possible for one's life.

God may have placed us in our families but he alone determines our identities.

In the eyes of his fellow Nazoreans, Jesus' life should not have amounted to what they were witnessing. After all, they had watched him grow up and knew his family well enough to name his mother and brothers. They knew that Jesus was not the son of a scholar but "the carpenter's son." When the townspeople processed all of this, they actually became offended by him. I don't know if the expression, "familiarity breeds contempt," was ever truer.

My friends, living a life where family is the basis for identity will surely be one marked by disappointment. We cannot let our own perceptions, or those of others, determine this for us. If Jesus lived this way, our world would be a lot different. People did not honor him for who he was because of who they thought he should be. His response to the offended was not one of disappointment or even offense. He simply conveyed the reality of how difficult it is for people who "know us" to embrace our "different," especially if it is beyond what they deem possible.

So, what was the basis for his identity?

How was Jesus able to break the ceiling others had placed on his life?

We find the answer earlier in Matthew:

[16]As soon as Jesus was baptized, he went up out of the water. At that moment heaven was opened, and he saw the Spirit of God descending like a dove and alighting on him. [17]And a voice from heaven said, "This is my Son, whom I love; with him I am well pleased." (Matthew 3:16-17)

Jesus' identity was firmly rooted in his relationship with the Father. He believed what the Father said about him – that he was his Son, that he was loved and how pleased the Father was with him – so much so that what others said about him fell on deaf ears. Though Jesus was likely aware of his unique identity in the Father's eyes prior to this moment, it is for our benefit, I believe, that he did not begin his ministry until after this recorded exchange. It is when we embrace who we are in the Father's eyes that we are able to truly live, doing so in the face of others' perceptions.

Maybe it should not be possible to be a doctor if you were raised by a drug dealer. Perhaps being a social worker does not quite make sense if you come from high society. When we embrace our identity as children of the Father, however, what is impossible becomes possible and what is nonsensical becomes a nonissue. What matters is who *he* says we are – we are his children. This means he loves us and is pleased with us. There are no accolades we need to amass for his validation; we can simply live in loving relationship with him.

Yes, Jesus was the "the carpenter's son." There is no shame in this, just as there is no shame in our own parentage. What should matter most to us is what in fact mattered most to him: being a child of the Father.

Our identity comes from him, and him alone.

CHAPTER 6:

"HONORING UNTIL THE END"

Though Jesus may have been a prophet without honor in his own home, this did not stop him from living honorably.

He was the kind of man who, despite his status, would treat people as he desired to be treated (Matthew 7:12). Prostitutes, tax collectors and sinners were drawn to him because he didn't look down upon them but desired to lift them up. While Jesus was disposed to honor all people, this was particularly the case when it came to Mary and Joseph.

We have examined how Jesus, as a 12-year-old with a growing relationship with the Father, returned to Nazareth with his parents and obeyed them. This early expression of submission would mark the rest of his life. He not only had healthy expectations of his parents but knew that honoring them would ultimately honor the Father.

How is this the case?

Most of us, I would assume, are familiar with the term, "the Ten Commandments." Some of you probably said to yourselves, "Yes! I saw that movie!" Thank you, again, Charlton Heston.

The Ten Commandments are, of course, what Moses received from God after epically leading the long captive Israelites out of Egypt. They were representative of how God wanted his people to live under his rule.

While there is something to glean from each of the 10, I specifically want to highlight every parent's favorite:

> *Honor your father and your mother, so that you may live long*
> *in the land the Lord your God is giving you.* (Exodus 20:12)

As a young Hebrew Jesus probably heard this portion of Scripture his fair share—as a young African American, I heard it a lot too. He knew that honoring his parents was a commandment directly from God. If Jesus were to not follow through on this, he would be deemed a lawbreaker, making him no different than a liar, thief or murderer. This would have been cataclysmic, with God's divine plan of redemption being completely undermined. Obeying his Father meant honoring his parents.

Jesus did not have perfect parents but this was of no consequence. As we have already established no one has perfect parents. The call to honor them, though, is just the same.

Are there any exceptions? Does drug addiction, alcoholism or simply poor judgment change things?

As difficult as these things are it does not seem so.

The serious Bible student may ask, "If Jesus fulfilled the law, do I still have to follow this commandment?" Paul has a good answer for you:

> [1]*Children, obey your parents in the Lord, for this is right.* [2] *"Honor*
> *your father and mother"—which is the first commandment with*
> *a promise* (Ephesians 6:1-2)

For any follower of Christ, honoring one's parents is an expectation. This is something Jesus modeled himself, as Luke draws our attention to his submission to Mary and Joseph as a boy. While this may be a given for a child, how does this look as an adult? How did Jesus model this when he transitioned to adulthood?

Sadly, Joseph fades from the scene as Jesus becomes a man. As such, the parent-child interactions we are privy to in his adult years are between him and Mary. There are two such interactions recorded in John's gospel that we will find beneficial in this regard. Here is the first:

> *¹On the third day a wedding took place at Cana in Galilee. Jesus' mother was there, ²and Jesus and his disciples had also been invited to the wedding. ³When the wine was gone, Jesus' mother said to him, "They have no more wine."*
>
> *⁴"Woman, why do you involve me?" Jesus replied. "My hour has not yet come."*
>
> *⁵His mother said to the servants, "Do whatever he tells you."*
> (John 2:1-5)

Weddings.

They are such a time of celebration and joy at the joining of two lives. In those days, however, the celebration ceased as soon as the wine ran out. We do not know how many days into the potential week-long feast we find this scene, but it was clear they had a problem on their hands.

Mary, perceptive as she was, noticed the wine was gone. Out of concern for the couple and the guests, who may have been relatives, she brings this to Jesus' attention. It is clear from this that Mary realized there was something special about Jesus. The solution to the problem would not be of natural means, and she knew her son had an inside track on the supernatural. While Jesus may have been special, he was still Mary's son, and she made *their* issue *his* issue.

Jesus' initial response to this is clear: he was hesitant to get involved at the risk of prematurely revealing his identity as the Messiah. Mary, nevertheless, persisted; she even involved the wedding servants. Moms sure do know how to give orders.

So, what did Jesus do? How did he honor Mary in this moment?

⁶Nearby stood six stone water jars, the kind used by the Jews for ceremonial washing, each holding from twenty to thirty gallons.

⁷Jesus said to the servants, "Fill the jars with water"; so they filled them to the brim.

⁸Then he told them, "Now draw some out and take it to the master of the banquet."

They did so, ⁹and the master of the banquet tasted the water that had been turned into wine. He did not realize where it had come from, though the servants who had drawn the water knew. Then he called the bridegroom aside ¹⁰and said, "Everyone brings out the choice wine first and then the cheaper wine after the guests have had too much to drink; but you have saved the best till now."

¹¹What Jesus did here in Cana of Galilee was the first of the signs through which he revealed his glory; and his disciples believed in him. (John 2:6-11)

Essentially, Jesus fulfilled her request in a way that did not compromise him. He reasoned there was a way to provide more wine without making the big reveal, and the key was actually the servants his mother involved. Only the servants (and his disciples) knew the source of the wine; the guests were completely unaware.

Based on Jesus' example, one of the ways we honor our parents as adults is fulfilling requests that are *within reason*. For Jesus, it was totally within his means to turn water into wine. It would only be reasonable, however, if his involvement was not to the detriment of his life and calling. He found a way to do both.

Had he not, this story would have ended much differently. If there had not been a way to provide the wine in secret, the guests would have just had to drink water. Mary might have been upset at this but Jesus would have been on firm footing. His timing is the Father's timing, and no parent's request has precedence over God's plan.

Parents, can we have a moment of honesty?

Sometimes our requests, expectations or even "demands" are *not reasonable.*

For instance, when your son marries he is to "leave father and mother and be joined to his wife" (Genesis 2:24 NKJV). To insist that your relationship with him is unchanged is not reasonable. You may not see, or speak with, him as frequently as before marriage. Some family traditions may need to be altered or even ended, depending on the direction of the family he has now established. If he is put in a position of needing to choose between you and his wife, he will (or at least should) choose his wife hands down. His wife is now his priority, and the implications of this should be accepted.

Paul, also, speaks to this notion of being reasonable when writing to the Ephesians. He says, "do not exasperate your children; instead, bring them up in the training and instruction of the Lord" (Ephesians 6:4). When it gets to the point where these requests become a source of legitimate frustration, the ability of a child to honor becomes hindered. As parents, we do not want to be a cause of contention but be an example, training and instructing our children in the ways of the Lord.

Can we ask things of our children? Yes; these requests, though, should be reasonable.

When met with a reasonable request, we honor our parents by fulfilling it. As an adult, it looks differently from cleaning our rooms, taking out the trash or brushing our teeth – if you live with your parents as an adult, nonetheless, these are still good practices. Honoring them could be helping financially in a way that does not result in personal financial strain. It could, also, mean assisting with a project, one that does not hinder responsibilities to work or family.

For Jesus, his mother asked him to remedy a major problem at probably the world's most famous wedding; interestingly enough, we do not know the names of the bride and groom. While history records his miraculous feat, let us also take note of his processing of this request. If the ultimate goal was to honor God, he could not fulfill Mary's request at the expense of doing so; an ill-timed public miracle would have not been congruent with the Father's plan for him. This is not meant to provide ammunition to question every request we receive from our parents. What we should do is have in view how honoring them points us in the direction of honoring the Father.

When this aligns, we would do well to fulfill these requests.

As we near the end of John's gospel, we find another scene that illustrates how Jesus showed honor to Mary:

> *[25]Near the cross of Jesus stood his mother, his mother's sister, Mary the wife of Clopas, and Mary Magdalene. [26]When Jesus saw his mother there, and the disciple whom he loved standing nearby, he said to her, "Woman, here is your son," [27]and to the disciple, "Here is your mother." From that time on, this disciple took her into his home. (John 19:25-27)*

A lot has happened since the wedding at Cana. Jesus amassed both a following and foes, as he was teaching, preaching and performing miracles all throughout Palestine. His rising popularity with the people did not translate to the religious establishment. Their criteria for a Messiah did not leave room for Jesus, and this meant getting rid of him. Upon his final visit to Jerusalem, the plot to put him to death reached its climax. The above scene finds him on the cross to which he was sentenced.

In his final moments, while in unimaginable pain, he looks and sees his mother.

I have to say, mothers have a way of always being there in the most painful moments of life. It is a tribute to their nature as nurturers.

Jesus realized what was happening to him would have ramifications for Mary. Obviously, there was the sorrow of losing a son, albeit temporarily. There was also the responsibility of caring for her. God has much to say about the care of widows in the Scriptures, especially when it is your own mother (1 Timothy 5:3-8).

Not looking very far from his mother, he sees "the disciple whom he loved," who we confidently conclude is John. He was the only of his disciples to appear at the cross, despite the risks of being associated with him; the others ran and in the case of Peter even denied knowing him. Jesus knew John was someone he could trust; someone his mother could trust. What ensues, then, is quite logical: Jesus entrusts the care of Mary to John.

It is nothing short of remarkable that Jesus, while dying, was able to give his attention to this. While nailed to the cross, hanging from his own skin and cartilage, every breath was at a premium and every word cost him more breath. For him to make this one of his final sayings speaks to the importance of honoring his mother. He could not even die without doing so one final time.

Jesus shows us that we, also, honor our parents by looking after their well-being. Even with brothers and sisters, he realized John was the best person to care for Mary. Not only had they not come to believe in him (yet) but Mary was 80 or so miles from Nazareth. She was in no condition to make the trip back home, and John was in a perfect position to look after her. Besides, by leaving for Nazareth, she would have missed out on all the post-resurrection festivities in Jerusalem.

There are times when we have to look out for our parents, even when they are not as concerned about themselves. Perhaps, due to health reasons, a parent needs to make a dietary change and is reluctant to do so. We can honor them by displaying our support of this new diet and strongly encouraging the change. Going grocery shopping for them, providing recipes and even preparing meals are ways to help care for them.

Like Mary, maybe you have a parent who has experienced loss. In her case, it was a spouse and now a child. While this has emotional realities for us, it also does for them. Somehow, Jesus mustered the strength, while on the cross, to look beyond his personal pain and attend to her. I am convinced God will give us this same strength when we resolved to similarly care for, and thus honor, our parents.

You may now be experiencing a time where your parent is in their final days. Growing old and dying is a part of life but it is still never easy. Caring for them looks differently, since it is not as much about preservation as it is comfort. In the case of a parent who has not followed the Lord, the most important thing we can do for them is ensure they know the God of all comfort. While their time on earth may be expiring, eternity with Jesus is awaiting them, should they receive this invitation to be with him forever. Though still difficult, it does bring us some solace to know they will spend their eternity in the presence of God.

My friends, we can summarize our conversation about this aspect of Jesus' life with one simple truth:

Through life's twists, turns, ups and downs,
God is calling us to honor our parents.

This has not always been easy for me. In fact, as I am writing this, I am looking back on my life and realizing all the ways that I have failed to do so. The good news is that it is never too late to adhere to this call to honor. It doesn't matter as much what has happened in the past but it matters the decision we make today. Each day, we simply continue to make this decision, which we know honors our Father.

We may sometimes wonder why God gifted us to our particular set of parents, but we can rest in the fact that his unique plan for our lives accounted for it. Jesus' time with his parents spanned from a manger in

Bethlehem to his final words from the cross – and God used it all. Our experiences, lessons and conversations are designed to contribute to our amazing journey with him. The journey we take in this life begins with our parents, and from time to time, this includes siblings too.

SECTION TWO:

"AN AMAZING BROTHER" – JESUS THE BROTHER

Matthew 13:55-56a

> [55] *"Isn't this the carpenter's son? Isn't his mother's name Mary, and aren't his brothers James, Joseph, Simon and Judas?* [56] *Aren't all his sisters with us?*

No, Jesus was not an only child.

In this way, he was not merely an individual runner but belonged to a team. Being a part of a team challenges us in unique ways, helping us run stronger and faster.

As we have discussed in brief, he had both brothers *and* sisters. I do not know if he could be truly "touched with the feeling of our infirmities" (Hebrews 4:15 KJV) if this was not the case. He knows what it is like to be a sibling surrounded by pigtails, and bedrooms that are pigsties; I'm pretty confident he kept his room clean though. Jesus is able to speak to those who grew up fighting for the bathroom, jockeying for use of the TV or negotiating for use of the family car – they, of course, did not have those things back then but you know what I mean.

Jesus shows us how managing our sibling relationships helps us to engage effectively with the world around us. While we do not have home videos or memoirs chronicling Jesus' family life, there are a few things the Scriptures reveal about his experience as a brother. This section, then, will explore how he related to his siblings and how this informs our own sibling relationships.

CHAPTER 7:

"BEING THE OLDEST"

Oh, the joys of having your first child.

The feeling of taking that precious baby in your hands for the first time is like none other. In awe, you stare at this tiny human being, recognizing the miracle you are holding; this is, of course, when you are not passed out from exhaustion.

Can those emotions ever be replicated?

For Mary and Joseph, the experience they had surrounding Jesus' birth would not be replicated...ever. His birth was the most unique in all history. Honestly, I think this is for the better. How would you handle a host of angels showing up at your hospital to serenade your baby?

Not only was his birth *amazing* but it was the first for Mary and Joseph. The couple, of course, did not consummate their marriage until after Jesus was born; Mary was not impregnated by her husband but by the Holy Spirit, as Matthew and Luke both tell us. With Jesus being their firstborn, they had experiences with him unique among their other children. One such instance was the deeply meaningful ceremony of dedicating him at the temple. Luke details the account:

> [22]*When the time came for the purification rites required by the Law of Moses, Joseph and Mary took him to Jerusalem to*

present him to the Lord [23] *(as it is written in the Law of the Lord,*
"Every firstborn male is to be consecrated to the Lord"), [24]*and*
to offer a sacrifice in keeping with what is said in the Law of the
Lord: "a pair of doves or two young pigeons." (Luke 2:22-24)

This tradition stemmed from the early days of God's people. Nearing the end of 430 years of slavery in Egypt, God's final plague upon the land would secure Israel's release: the death of the firstborn. The Israelites were exempted from this plague by applying the blood of a lamb unto their doorposts, which is commemorated by the Passover. God also instituted the consecration of the firstborn male as a reminder that he had spared each of Israel's firstborn during this time. As a parent participating in this ceremony, you were basically saying that your son belonged to God.

While this was especially true for Mary and Joseph, there is an underlying sentiment for all of us. When you have your first child, there is so much you do not know. There is constant questioning, second-guessing, experimenting and the anxiety of trying to keep this human being alive. Truly, perhaps in a different way than with our other children, we have to give our first over to God.

In the case of the child, though, they reap the results of this emotionally charged period in the life of the parent. When conversing with other parents, there is always a concession of being more relaxed after having child number two. For number one, this often means tighter reigns. Indeed, there are things siblings will be able to do that maybe were not allowed in the case of the oldest, like playing in the dirt or staying up late.

Did the rules change?

Not necessarily. It was the emphasis that probably did.

Every parent will convey equal love for their children but would have to concede different treatment, especially in the case of the oldest. Simply based on being around the longest, there are expectations of them not congruent with the others. The oldest is the presumed leader of the pack and is expected to set an example. If you've ever experienced getting in trouble for what someone else did, you know what I mean.

There are, however, blessings associated with being the firstborn. In Hebrew tradition, the oldest son would receive a "double portion" of his father's inheritance (Deuteronomy 21:17) by way of birthright. This was so coveted in the days of old that younger siblings were willing to scheme to take it for themselves (Genesis 25:31). More important than material gain, though, is the quality time one was able to spend with their parents before the arrival of siblings. From family to family, this window of time varies in length; for some it's ten years, for some five years or perhaps just one. Regardless, this is a special time of connection, milestones and growth, for both parent and child.

These blessings, also, extend beyond this only child period. As the firstborn, you are able to see the journey of your siblings unfold from the beginning. Without fail, kids always fall in love with their newly arrived brother or sister. One of the greatest sights in life is seeing an older sibling show affection to the new baby in the home. The tenderness of that moment is enough to melt even the hardest heart. We do not have this on record but I can imagine the joy Jesus experienced at the arrival of each of his siblings.

On this subject, our gleaning from Jesus' life really comes to us by way of reminder:

As the oldest, you must keep in mind the blessing of being gifted to your parents first, while also owning the unique responsibility of being the senior sibling.

Yes, there is a unique dynamic to being first. At times, you may experience what Jesus said on one occasion during his ministry: "So the last will be first, and the first will be last" (Matthew 20:16). You probably even had the thought, "My parents treat my youngest sibling like a baby." Sometimes, of course, your youngest sibling is actually a baby. There are times, even still, when you are reminded of the significance of your special place in the family.

We took note of this scene in John's gospel but we'll return to it in order to see how this was the case in Jesus' life:

> [25]*Near the cross of Jesus stood his mother, his mother's sister, Mary the wife of Clopas, and Mary Magdalene.* [26]*When Jesus saw his mother there, and the disciple whom he loved standing nearby, he said to her, "Woman, here is your son,"* [27]*and to the disciple, "Here is your mother." From that time on, this disciple took her into his home.* (John 19:25-27)

Again, Jesus is hanging from the cross. With the weight (and sins) of the world on his shoulders, he gives his attention to the care of his mother, Mary. While we noted how honorable this gesture of our Lord's was, could it be that he felt a sense of responsibility? After all, Joseph was gone, which now made Jesus the male authority in his family. It is, also, worth noting that Mary's sister was present at the cross. Couldn't she have cared for Mary?

In Jesus' estimation, this was not a job for his aunt. Given the present circumstances, this was not even a job for his siblings. He took the lead on caring for her, making on-the-fly arrangements for her to stay with John. Jesus embraced this as his responsibility, and in fulfilling it, he sets an example for all of those born first. This example is one of supporting one's parent(s) and being a model for one's siblings.

Being the oldest does have its pressures but also has some privileges. Maybe there have been times when you have acted as a moderator between your parents and siblings. The feeling of being between a rock and a hard place is never fun but there is a silver lining. That you were able to occupy this position in the first place speaks of the influence you have in your family.

Pressure and privilege.

Perhaps you decided to go away to college when this time came in your life. Even still, it could have been the case that the hopes of the first degree in the family rested on your shoulders. Each class session, each grade and each semester carry so much weight. Add to this the void of advice in keeping with being a trailblazer, as well as any financial challenges and you have yourself a pressure-filled four years of schooling. Then came the day when you walked across the stage. Not only was this a deeply gratifying moment for you but also your family. How proud must they have been to watch this journey – your journey – culminate in such a rewarding way.

Pressure and privilege.

Like Jesus, perhaps you did lose a parent. This is a time of deep sadness for all involved. There are, nevertheless, decisions needing to be made, arrangements needing coordination and people who need to be notified. It is likely your surviving parent only had the strength to grieve. Your siblings, while present physically, may not have been as much emotionally. Looking at the work needing to be done to honor the memory of your beloved parent, you probably took the reins on all the planning. While a great source of stress, taking on this responsibility surely brought comfort to all those who loved your mother or father. They will not soon forget the support you were to the entire family during this time.

Pressure and privilege.

The experience of each firstborn is by no means the same. What is shared, though, is the opportunity to have a Jesus-sized impact on your entire family. This impact will be actualized when receiving in your heart God's desire for you to be born first. Surely, this is his blessing to you and your entire family.

CHAPTER 8:

"GOOD TIMES"

Blessings, it can seem, come few and far between for certain families.

One family, in particular, who comes to mind is the Evans family. No, they are not my relatives. Neither are they neighbors from childhood. They, technically, are not even real.

The Evans' are a fictional family from the 1970's sitcom, *Good Times*. As an African American family living in the projects of inner-city Chicago, they encountered challenges that gripped the heart and conveyed the sobering realities of many who could, and still can, relate. While times may have been tough for the family, they seemed to have a special appreciation for moments of celebration. In fact, the difficulty in their lives is what made these moments more meaningful. The things typically considered "small" were for them quite "big." Making a bill payment, for instance, was worthy of a party; it would, of course, need to be an inexpensive one.

It would seem the Evans family and Jesus' family have a few things in common. In both cases, there were two parents in the home but eventually the father passes away. Also, each family had multiple children of both genders. Lastly, both families knew what it meant to struggle financially.

Though his lineage was one of royalty, Jesus did not come from means. As this section's opening excerpt from Matthew reminds us, his father was a carpenter by trade. We have a certain framework for this vocation today but being a carpenter meant something much different for Joseph, especially while living in a small town in the first century. This is how one commentator describes it:

> *In the cities the carpenters would be Greeks, and skilled work-*
> *men; the carpenter of a provincial village could only have held a*
> *very humble position, and secured a very moderate [income].*[18]

Joseph did not live in the big city of Jerusalem, or any city for that matter. He and his family settled in the humble town of Nazareth. Nathanael, who eventually became a follower of Jesus, commented, "Nazareth! Can anything good come from there?" (John 1:46a). Living there did not seem to give anyone an advantage in life, and certainly not economically. Feeding Jesus, his four brothers and, at least, three sisters (this is supposed by the use of the world "all" in Matthew 13:56) would have been a challenge for anyone but especially Joseph.

The financial reality for Jesus' family is first made known at his dedication in the temple. If you recall, Luke says Mary and Joseph offered "a sacrifice in keeping with what is said in the Law of the Lord: 'a pair of doves or two young pigeons'" (Luke 2:24). This offering was actually on Mary's behalf, which was for her purification after childbirth. Unable to afford the standard offering, they took advantage of a provision in the Law for those in their shoes:

> *But if she cannot afford a lamb, she is to bring two doves or*
> *two young pigeons, one for a burnt offering and the other for*
> *a sin offering. In this way the priest will make atonement for*
> *her, and she will be clean. (Leviticus 12:8)*

From the onset, it was clear Jesus' family would not live in the lap of luxury. The one eventually crowned King of kings and Lord of lords grew up in

---

18   Farrar, F. W. (2013). *Life of Christ*. Theclassics Us.

modest circumstances, sharing with his brothers and sisters while doing so. A family of at least 10 living on a carpenter's wage, most assuredly, meant some kind of strain on the household; Jesus and his siblings were, perhaps, employed rather early on in life to help make ends meet.

The presence of tough times, though, did not mean the absence of good times. They still traveled to Jerusalem, the Disneyland of the Hebrews, to celebrate the Passover every year (Luke 2:41). It seems they also traveled there for the yearly Feast of Tabernacles (John 7:2-10). We know they attended weddings (John 2:1). If difficulty was going to stop any family from living life, it would not be them.

Of all of the families God the Father could have placed his Son, he chose the household of Joseph and Mary. Yes, Jesus was the firstborn but after a while, things started to get a little crowded. He would receive less and less attention, while amassing more and more responsibility, living very humbly all the while.

Did this bother Jesus?

It doesn't seem so.

In fact, during his ministry he espoused a special place in his and the Father's heart for the poor (Luke 6:20). His upbringing helped to shape his calling, and even his perspective as to the important things in life. He did not spend his time pursuing wealth, instead being generous to the people whom he loved. What we can glean from Jesus, then, is this:

Having means is not more important than having family.

This lesson is one taught to us from time-to-time. Losing a loved one reminds us that we cannot put a price on the time we've spent, and wish we still had with them. There are even moments when we are faced with a choice that would advance our careers but also mean less time with family. Says

Harold Kushner, "No one ever said on their deathbed 'I wish I'd spent more time at the office.'"[19]

Ironically, we perhaps best learn this lesson from those we would consider successful. Hearing some of these people entering their twilight years and voicing their regrets, almost always including family, is a sobering reminder for those of us who are still building our lives. Paul McCartney, former lead vocalist for The Beatles, expressed that he'd go back and spend more time with his mother when asked what he would do if he had a time machine – he was 14 when she passed. Even the late Billy Graham, dubbed "America's Pastor," conceded he would "spend more time at home with my family, and I'd study more and preach less."[20]

Family was quite important in Jesus' culture. N.T. Wright, a New Testament theologian and Anglican bishop, comments, "The sense of family identity among the Jews was a central and vital symbol," also adding "family and hence national identity mattered supremely."[21] Family may have been supreme but this did not make them exempt from the relational strain caused by money or the lack thereof. In fact, while Jesus is teaching on one occasion, one person takes the opportunity to try and have Jesus resolve a family squabble:

> [13]*Someone in the crowd said to him, "Teacher, tell my brother to divide the inheritance with me." [14]Jesus replied, "Man, who appointed me a judge or an arbiter between you?" 15Then he said to them, "Watch out! Be on your guard against all kinds*

19   Engel, J. (2020, May 04). Council post: The 10 commandment of highly Effective LEADERSHIP: Live a balanced and fulfilling life. Retrieved February 24, 2021, from https://www.forbes.com/sites/forbescoachescouncil/2020/05/04/the-10 -commandment-of-highly-effective-leadership-live-a-balanced-and-fulfilling-life/?sh=7867f9a730ad

20   Gregoire, C. (2017, December 07). What 8 highly successful people wish they had done differently. Retrieved May 24, 2020, from https://www.huffpost.com/entry/successful-people-mistakes_n_3829864

21   Wright, N. T. (2021). *The Challenge of Jesus: Rediscovering Who Jesus Was and Is.* Intervarsity Press.

of greed; life does not consist in an abundance of possessions."
(Luke 12:13-15)

Speaking of regrets, I bet you that guy wished he had never called out to Jesus from the crowd. The ensuing parable that Jesus tells the listening audience, inspired by this man, was a sobering one to say the least (Luke 12:16-21). Jesus addresses the impact our disposition towards money can have on our relationships, even with our own brother. This is a lesson we should very much take to heart.

Jesus does not strike me as a guy who had any regrets. Instead, he is the only person who with absolute certainty can say he did everything he intended. You would not make the declaration, "it is finished" (John 19:30), if this was not the case. It seems, then, he can look back on the decisions he made regarding his family and express this confidence. No, he did not grow up with means but his wealth was in his relationships, formatively his family.

From the onset, it was clear Jesus' family was one that would follow the God of their ancestors. Not only did this mean maintaining the rituals and traditions but also being people committed to the Scripture. Hearing from the Torah, the prophets and psalms was commonplace for any Hebrew child, especially when attending synagogue every week. Upon hearing Proverbs read, I'm sure Jesus identified with the following verse:

Better a small serving of vegetables with love than a fattened calf with hatred. (Proverbs 15:17)

Which is more important: a fattened calf, representing opulence and luxury, or love?

The answer, brothers and sisters, is quite clear.

On a carpenter's budget, it is likely that dinner for Jesus' family looked more like a small serving of vegetables rather than a calf, much less a fattened one. The love their family had or any of our families has for one another, yet, is what truly makes for a happy home. Having means is great but our priority should be building memories and relationships marked by love. Only this kind of building will be able to endure moments of difficulty or even disappointment.

CHAPTER 9:

"SIBLING DISAPPOINTMENT"

When I think of what it means to be a sibling, at the top of the list is having your brother or sister's back.

Through thick and thin, you can always count on your siblings to be there for you. During a break-up, health challenge or even financial difficulty, they remain a stabilizing force that gives us the courage to keep going. It is clear the writer of Proverbs had this in mind when he penned, "A friend loves at all times, and a brother is born for a time of adversity" (Proverbs 17:17).

Again, I do not have siblings biologically. I am fortunate, even so, to have friends who have loved me at all times and been a brother to me during the most difficult seasons of my life. One of these people is my friend, Mike.

It seems to me, each of us has at least one person in our lives who is around for what I'd like to call, "Charles Dickens moments." In *A Tale of Two Cities*, Dickens famously writes, "It was the best of times, it was the worst of times." Mike has been there for the happiest of moments, none more special than my wedding day. It is during the difficult seasons, though, where our brotherhood was truly forged.

As I was entering my senior year of undergrad, I ran into a financial wall. Not only did I have a balance I could not afford to pay but this also meant I was unable to arrange for housing on campus during the summer

– I had no place to go. In typical Mike fashion, he offered for me to live with him, rent free, which ended up being for the duration of the ensuing school year.

The catch?

I had to share a small studio with him and another person for the entire time. Needless to say, we became quite close through this experience.

There is an inherent sense that our brothers and sisters can be counted on. No matter what the situation, we have an inner witness that says, "I know my siblings will be there for me." This, of course, makes it all the more painful when it is not the case. As I'm sure you deduced, Jesus can relate to this.

> [1]*After this, Jesus went around in Galilee. He did not want to go about in Judea because the Jewish leaders there were looking for a way to kill him.* [2]*But when the Jewish Festival of Tabernacles was near,* [3]*Jesus' brothers said to him, "Leave Galilee and go to Judea, so that your disciples there may see the works you do.* [4]*No one who wants to become a public figure acts in secret. Since you are doing these things, show yourself to the world."* [5]*For even his own brothers did not believe in him.*
>
> [6]*Therefore Jesus told them, "My time is not yet here; for you any time will do.* [7]*The world cannot hate you, but it hates me because I testify that its works are evil.* [8]*You go to the festival. I am not going up to this festival, because my time has not yet fully come."* 9*After he had said this, he stayed in Galilee.*
> (John 7:1-9)

So much for moral support.

Jesus, by this time, had established a reputation. Some lauded him as a prophet sent from God, while others saw him as a fraud and a threat; as you just read, the Jewish leaders were plotting to take his life. Having retreated to his home turf, likely expecting to find refuge amongst his family, he was instead met by criticism. It is unclear whether or not Jesus' brothers knew his life was in danger but their lack of concern is apparent.

I am not quite sure what made Jesus' brothers say what they did to him. Was it jealousy? They clearly had a sense of his aptitude for the miraculous. Perhaps they were saying to themselves, "If we could do what he can do, this is what we would do." Clearly, his brothers did not agree with the way he was going about things.

I wonder how this made Jesus feel? It wasn't enough that his mother and brothers had previously tried to put a stop to his ministry; their lack of support persisted through perhaps one of the most stressful times in his life. Aren't these the times for which brothers were born? Maybe his sisters shared similar sentiments but we all know how vocal sisters can be; this is, oftentimes, for the better. I had a group of female friends in college who were like sisters to me. It is because of their persistence that I stopped wearing my holey sweatpants to class every day and began to dress decently. Starting to care about my attire, I believe, is one of the reasons I am now married.

You expect your siblings to have your back but especially your brother. When some bully is picking on you at school, it is typically your brother that comes to the rescue. Brothers stand up for each other, protect each other and, if necessary, fight for each other. We are our brother's keeper.

There are times, still, when brothers do not see eye-to-eye. These disagreements may be over choice of girlfriend (hopefully, not choice of spouse), a financial decision or choice of vocation. Jesus' vocation was to be Israel's messiah, and he had a distinct sense of how this undertaking would be fulfilled. Not only did his brothers call his tactics into question but they just did not believe in him.

How do we persist with the most important, maybe even most difficult, things in our lives without the support of our siblings? What can we glean from Jesus' life to navigate this?

Validation doesn't come from our siblings but the one who sent us.

Jesus had an uncanny sense of mission, one that would not be deterred by the opinions of others, even those related to him. He was resolved to do the Father's will at all costs, which meant he had to make peace with being disappointed. It was probably difficult for Jesus to have perfect strangers willing to follow him but not have his own brothers believe in him. Despite all they had seen, for them, it was not enough. Even for you reading this right now, you may feel your best efforts have not been enough to garner the affirmation of your siblings.

What will it take?

Trick question.

Again, our validation does not come from our siblings, or anyone else for that matter. Yes, we should have people in our lives who encourage us; Jesus, of course, had his disciples (more on this later). Living for the Father, though, means seeking *his* validation. When this is in view, we can truly navigate any criticism, dissonance or lack of support, just as Jesus did. Our story continues:

> [10]*However, after his brothers had left for the festival, he went also, not publicly, but in secret. . .* [14]*Not until halfway through the festival did Jesus go up to the temple courts and begin to teach.* [15]*The Jews there were amazed and asked, "How did this man get such learning without having been taught?"*
>
> [16]*Jesus answered, "My teaching is not my own. It comes from the one who sent me.* [17]*Anyone who chooses to do the will of God will find out whether my teaching comes from God or whether I speak on my own.* [18]*Whoever speaks on their own does so to gain personal glory, but he who seeks the glory of the one who sent him is a man of truth; there is nothing false about him.* (John 7:10, 14-18)

Jesus sought the glory of the one who sent him; he did not speak on his own. Initially, he did not go to the festival with his brothers because he was not trying to make a name for himself. Yes, Jesus' calling demanded that he was a public figure, but he did not want them to get the impression that he actually agreed with their methods. His timing was not his brothers' timing, it was the Father's timing, and he would not be pressured into making a decision to appease them.

Sometimes, however, we can experience conflict in our hearts because we do not know whose will we are doing. Is it the Father's? Is it our brother's? Or is it our own? Pursing the will of the Father is what satisfies the need for others to validate us.

Do you know the will of God for your life? There is, perhaps, nothing more important than following Paul's advice to us: "Don't act thoughtlessly, but understand what the Lord wants you to do" (Ephesians 5:17 NLT). When we prayerfully discern his purpose for us, a lack of support is viewed less as a personal indictment and more a misalignment with God's will, at least for our lives.

Yes, it is so life-giving when our siblings show their support of our pursuits. Our focus, though, should be the life the Father gives. Truly, "whoever does the will of God lives forever" (1 John 2:17b).

CHAPTER 10:

"ALWAYS COMMITTED"

In life, disappointment is all but guaranteed.

When siblings are the culprit, it is a tough pill to swallow. If this disappointment persists over time, as in the case of Jesus, it can become discouraging. Having the affirmation of outsiders and not that of your own brothers can even cause one to withdraw.

Still, there are other things that surface in sibling relationships that can challenge their very existence. This could be betraying a confidence, reckless words or even an altercation.

Have these things ever happened to you?

Relationships, certainly ones that are lifelong, have ebbs and flows. Perhaps the writer of Ecclesiastes best conveys these "seasons" of life (Ecclesiastes 3:1-8). If these seasons change as often as he says, relationships have to weather a great deal. Sure, there is laughter and celebration but also the inevitable moments of pain and heartache. Yes, in these adverse times we need our brothers but let us not forget how much they also need us.

Jesus had come into the world for a purpose: "For the Son of Man came to seek and to save the lost" (Luke 19:10). Clearly, though, this was a purpose his brothers did not perceive. To them, Jesus was himself lost, and not in a position to save anyone. In this case, the words found in the opening chapter of John's gospel have never been truer: "He came to that which was his own, but his own did not receive him" (John 1:11).

The natural thing to do in response would be to simply give up. After all, "there is a time to embrace and a time to refrain from embracing" (Ecclesiastes 3:5b). Why continue to try to embrace people who refuse to do the same? Should we be expected to allow our hearts to be broken again and again? Even the apostle Paul, a Hebrew of Hebrews, found occasion for bailing on his Jewish brothers:

> *5When Silas and Timothy came from Macedonia, Paul devoted himself exclusively to preaching, testifying to the Jews that Jesus was the Messiah. 6But when they opposed Paul and became abusive, he shook out his clothes in protest and said to them, "Your blood be on your own heads! I am innocent of it. From now on I will go to the Gentiles."* (Acts 18:5-6)

We have all had moments where we've expressed, "enough is enough," but it must have taken a lot for arguably the greatest Christian to give up preaching to his own. Was this also the case with Jesus?

Though Jesus was rejected, he continued with his mission, which was ultimately for the benefit of those turning him away. His brothers may not have known how much they needed him but he knew. It was his love for them, and the rest of the world, which led him to the cross to die for their sins. What happens when he rises triumphantly from the grave may actually be most telling of his brotherly commitment.

First Corinthians chapter 15 is one of the hallmark passages of the New Testament. In it, Paul gives probably the most thorough treatment of the resurrection known to man. The Corinthian Christians, to whom he writes, had actually started to believe there was no such thing as resurrection from the dead. Fundamentally, he debunks this notion by using the most obvious illustration: Jesus himself. Says Paul, "if Christ has not been raised, our preaching is useless and so is your faith" (1 Corinthians 15:14).

As the apostle defends his position, he even goes to the length of providing a list of people to whom Jesus appeared after rising from the dead. After all, who could argue with eyewitness testimony? The list he provides is as follows:

> *3For what I received I passed on to you as of first importance: that Christ died for our sins according to the Scriptures, 4that he was buried, that he was raised on the third day according to the Scriptures, 5and that he appeared to Cephas, and then to the Twelve. 6After that, he appeared to more than five hundred of the brothers and sisters at the same time, most of whom are still living, though some have fallen asleep. 7Then he appeared to James, then to all the apostles, 8and last of all he appeared to me also, as to one abnormally born.* (1 Corinthians 15:3-8)

Of course, if you want people to carry on a message based on your own resurrection, you should probably give those messengers proof of life. He, in turn, does this for Peter, the Twelve apostles, a group of 500 disciples and Paul. What is interesting to find in this list is Jesus' personal appearance to his brother, James.

We do not know much about the time and circumstances of this appearance. In fact, this passage is the only mention of the post-resurrection meeting between the two. What we do know is that James had not believed in Jesus, seemingly until this encounter. James would go on to be an influential figure in the church, reaching a status on par with the apostles – our Bibles have a letter that bears his name. Things did not start this way, though.

I do not think anyone would have predicted James' fate, including James himself. Peter and the gang may have been on the "Jesus Christ" bandwagon but not him. To he and his brothers, Jesus was more of a "mess" than a "messiah." Jesus, nevertheless, would not be deterred by James' disdain. He, quite literally, went to hell and back for the sake of his brother's future, for the sake of his eternity. Far be it from Jesus to have given up on someone he loved.

My friends, Jesus teaches us a difficult, yet powerful lesson by how he responds to his brothers:

We are to never give up on our siblings.

When Jesus' brothers left for the Feast of Tabernacles without him, they essentially staged a walkout. At a time when families were united to celebrate their heritage as Hebrews, James and the gang did not feel the need to bring along their older brother. It, also, didn't matter to them that Jesus, as an adult male, would actually be in violation of the Law by not attending (Deuteronomy 16:16). They had grown tired of his antics and, perhaps, did not want to have anything to do with this would-be savior. After their exchange in John 7, the Scripture does not record an interaction between Jesus and his brothers prior to his death.

Sadly, some siblings do not have the opportunity to repair their relationships. If allowed, bitterness, offense and grudges can last for years. Before you know it, you can be standing next to a hospital bed or casket, saying the things you wished you would've said while your brother or sister could still hear them. Maybe this was the case with Jesus' brothers?

Staying committed means that we do not give up. We do not want to be those who, like Pilate, wash our hands of people. Even when distance becomes necessary, for the health of the relationship and everyone involved, our hearts should have a steadfast desire to see things made right and for the very best to come to pass. Letting go does not mean giving up; sometimes, this may be needed for our siblings to become who God has intended.

Even in the case of the apostle Paul, he realized that his Jewish brothers would not come to know Jesus if he did not turn is evangelistic pursuits toward the Gentiles. Yes, the Acts 18 incident in Corinth definitely angered him – he had a right to be angry! His heart, though, was not one of abandonment but disappointment. Paul conveys his commitment when he writes the following:

> *¹I speak the truth in Christ—I am not lying, my conscience confirms it through the Holy Spirit—²I have great sorrow and unceasing anguish in my heart. ³For I could wish that I myself were cursed and cut off from Christ for the sake of my people, those of my own race, ⁴the people of Israel. (Romans 9:1-4a)*

> *Inasmuch as I am the apostle to the Gentiles, I take pride in my ministry ¹⁴in the hope that I may somehow arouse my own people to envy and save some of them. (Romans 11:13b-14)*

Sometimes, the challenge with remaining committed is not a lack of forbearance but a lack of hope. If you have been persevering for years with no apparent change, this starts to wear on you. The prospect of things turning for the better can start to look bleaker, making more tenuous the desire to hold out.

With God, though, there is always hope.

One person in my life who always has a hopeful outlook is my brother-in-law, Matt. Matt is just someone you always want around. He is a constant source of encouragement and believes the best of everyone. There was a time when his sister, Elise, was not walking with the Lord. The path she had chosen to take led her to a relationship with someone that was far from life-giving, to say the least. Despite the reoccurring conversations about the negatives of the relationship, things remain unchanged. While it was difficult for him to see this persist in her life, Matt remained prayerfully committed. By God's grace, Elise is now a follower of Christ and is married to a wonderful man of God.

I think this bears repeating: with God, there is always hope. As long as he remains part of the equation, there is no relational hurdle that cannot be overcome, no wound that cannot be healed and no heart that is unable to change. Just ask Jesus.

While his brothers had, previously, tried to put a stop to his ministry, as well as issue their scathing criticism, the post-resurrection account of the story of Jesus paints quite a different picture. James, as we previously noted, is visited by Jesus at a time unknown to us. It is uncertain if Jesus visited his other brothers, but we do know they all had a similar change of heart. Luke writes:

> [12]*Then the apostles returned to Jerusalem from the hill called the Mount of Olives, a Sabbath day's walk from the city.* [13]*When they arrived, they went upstairs to the room where they were staying. Those present were Peter, John, James and Andrew; Philip and Thomas, Bartholomew and Matthew; James son of Alphaeus and Simon the Zealot, and Judas son of James.* [14]*They all joined together constantly in prayer, along with the women and Mary the mother of Jesus, and with his brothers.* (Acts 1:12-14)

Yes, Jesus' brothers were numbered among the earliest post-resurrection followers of Jesus. They may have missed the feeding of the 5,000 and the raising of Lazarus but they were there for the outpouring of the Holy Spirit at Pentecost. Why? Because Jesus remained committed to them.

Sure, the claims of their brother were proven true by his resurrection. Still, not everyone's response was one of belief. As Matthew records, when the disciples saw Jesus, some worshiped and some doubted (Matthew 28:17). Even then, this belief is not simply in a dead man who is now alive but one who would experience death in the first place because of his undying commitment to those whom he loves. That he would remain committed after being vindicated is probably most impressive.

Whatever you do, don't give up on your siblings. Even if things look "dead," relationally speaking, there is resurrection power available. This power turns fights into forgiveness, avoidance into availability and doubt into devotion.

How amazing is that?

SECTION THREE:

"AN AMAZING FRIEND" – JESUS THE FRIEND

John 15:12-15

> [12] *My command is this: Love each other as I have loved you.* [13]*Greater love has no one than this: to lay down one's life for one's friends.* [14] *You are my friends if you do what I command.* [15] *I no longer call you servants, because a servant does not know his master's business. Instead, I have called you friends, for everything that I learned from my Father I have made known to you.*

Seldom has anyone crossed the finish line without a cheering section.

Our lives are most well-lived when we have the companionship, comfort and encouragement of those who have expressed an unwavering commitment. We need friends but we will only have them if we tend to those relationships.

What was it like to be Jesus' friend? Was he easygoing? Did others find it tough to keep up with him in conversations? Were the people in his circle constantly intimidated? The giving of advice surely was a one-way street.

More importantly, Jesus had friends, which reinforces the great need for them. Indeed, a man will go only as far as his friendships allow. He recognized, though, the longevity of these relationships would be upon the strength of his labor, loyalty and love. His example shows us growing our friendships is paramount to enabling mutual edification and influence.

If he was even remotely as committed of a friend as he was a brother, we know we are looking in the right place for an example of true friendship. From his friendships, then, we seek to learn what it means to be a *real* friend.

CHAPTER 11:

"QUALITY TIME"

I, for one, do not espouse to be the greatest friend in the world.

Yes, I try to sincerely love the people in my life. I give the best advice that I can, though I've probably received better advice than I've given over the years. If a friend is in need, I will lend a helping hand.

The thing that always seems to get me, nonetheless, is not really spending time with my friends. I am notorious for being the one that is too busy to hangout or even for a phone call. (For my friends reading this, try to tone down your "amen.") We all have people in our lives who have been with us through "thick and thin," with whom we have great memories; I, for one, feel most privileged in this way. Friendships, however, are not based on past experiences alone. It is through spending time together any relationship is truly nourished and grown. I cannot tell you how many times I have reconnected with a friend and thought, "Why didn't I do this sooner?"

While your experience may not be as extreme as mine, I am convinced we can all relate to this to some degree. The pace of life can often present a challenge to us investing in our most significant relationships, especially in Western culture. As a single person, this was already a hurdle to climb. Add a spouse, children, work, school and other responsibilities and you may be inclined to think, "Who could keep up with friendships amidst the swirling winds of life?"

If I were to give you one guess, I'm confident you would answer correctly.

Let us remind ourselves that despite the importance of our jobs, the fullness of our calendars and the size of our families, there is no one who was as busy as Jesus. Again, his friend John writes, "Jesus did many other things as well. If every one of them were written down, I suppose that even the whole world would not have room for the books that would be written" (John 21:25).

Though Jesus was often busy, he managed to make time for his friends. I say, "make time," because for many of us these interactions do not just fall into our laps; they have to be created. Truthfully, you can even be with someone and not really reap the benefit of their company. From responding to work messages to attempting to discretely watch the restaurant television, many of our interactions have been undermined by these distractions.

Recognizing the pace of his life and the urgency of his calling, Jesus simply invited people into what he was doing. He was clear that the responses to his invitation would vary, but those who received it wholeheartedly would gain much more than a rabbi. As this section's opening passage suggests, he was certainly the Master. He had the wisdom and authority to issue commands to those who pledged to follow him. After walking together for almost three years, Jesus has a DTR ("define the relationship") talk with his disciples. Yes, they were to still call him "Lord," but he clarifies that he sees them not just as servants but also friends.

The merit of this friendship, though, was the time they spent together. Jesus was able to reveal the master's business to the disciples because they remained with him, when times were good and not so good. They had shared experiences and memories, not merely because they were privileged witnesses to the greatest life ever lived but also Jesus' constant invitation to join him on his amazing journey.

John conveys Jesus' intentionality as he chronicles a particular instance in his early ministry:

After this, Jesus and his disciples went out into the Judean countryside, where he spent some time with them, and baptized. (John 3:22)

While baptizing was certainly an important thing to do, just as important to Jesus was carving out time to spend with his friends. He recognized the need for quality time, especially amidst the demands of life and ministry. Jesus was not merely concerned with his disciples' productivity; there also needed to be depth of relationship. In the long run, their productivity would not be sustained by a drive to excel but a commitment to a person. For Jesus, this was cultivated by being intentional with setting aside time and with how the time was actually spent.

Here is what we can take from Jesus to help our own friendships:

As friends, we have to be intentional.

Truly, Jesus was deliberate about everything he did. When traveling, he purposefully selected the path he would take, even if he was making a trip he did often (John 4:3-4). A person may have had the same condition as someone he previously healed, but he did not necessarily heal them the same way. Regarding those closest to him, his words, actions and investments were hardly arbitrary.

In our desire to act, think and live like him, our friends should benefit from the same degree of intention. This is not to say relationships should at all be scripted. We cannot even predict what will happen tomorrow, so this approach would surely come up empty. Each of us can recall unplanned instances where we spent time with friends that we hold dear. For me, one such time was when attending a Super Bowl party at a friend's house. Chicago winters can be brutal, and it certainly was the case on this night. An overwhelming amount of snow made a commute back home almost impossible, and that's if you could even dig out your car! The Super Bowl party, then, became a slumber party. I still laugh just thinking about it.

There, though, is as much room for proactivity as there is spontaneity. While having unplanned adventures is always fun, I have found the planned ones just as much, if not more, gratifying. One of my favorite memories involves the men who stood beside me on my wedding day. In light of my affinity for Marvel© movies, I purchased tickets for all of us to see *Avengers: Infinity War* as a token of my appreciation for them – you're really missing out if you haven't seen it. I did not know it was possible for grown men to act so much like children. We joked, laughed and carried on like we didn't have a care in the world; we, also, raided the concession stand like a group of teenagers. Honestly, it was more fun than my bachelor party.

Being intentional means we are seeking opportunities to advance in our relationships with one another. Doing so on one occasion is great but we must continue to do so if we truly want to see our friendships grow. Fittingly, Mark lets us know that Jesus' friendly gesture in John's gospel was not a one-time occurrence:

> [30]*The apostles gathered around Jesus and reported to him all they had done and taught.* [31]*Then, because so many people were coming and going that they did not even have a chance to eat, he said to them, "Come with me by yourselves to a quiet place and get some rest."* (Mark 6:30-31)

Jesus was busy. The apostles were busy. People were so hungry for their ministry that they did not even have time to eat. I am sure you know what it is like to be so busy at work you neglect eating lunch.

It became apparent to Jesus that he and his companions needed quality time together…again. Yes, it can be difficult to make this time but we have to try. With the pace of our lives, things change so quickly. There is one close friend of mine, who at the time of this writing lives walking distance from me. So much time had passed between hangouts that he and his then pregnant wife, who already had a two-year old, now also had a four-month old baby. To make matters worse, he was one of my groomsmen. (I told you I had a hard time with this.)

The example of Jesus is not meant to be an unattainable standard; remember, he is able to empathize with our weaknesses (Hebrews 4:15). Interestingly enough, after Jesus tries to get away with the disciples, he actually runs into a large crowd. Even his attempt for quality time was inundated by the demands of life. Truly, it happens to the best of us.

While they did not have alone time as planned, what ensues is the feeding of the 5,000. If you recall, this miracle is the only one recorded in all four gospels, aside from Jesus rising from the dead. This memory was so impactful that Matthew, John and Peter (relaying his account to his ministry associate, Mark) all thought it worth recounting to the entire world; Luke, who later becomes a follower of Christ, follows suit. I think if we interviewed the disciples, they would concede that having this memory of serving 5,000 people with Jesus is greater than the limited time they would have had alone. Besides, after everyone was fed, there remained 12 baskets full of leftovers, one for each hungry disciple.

It is not that our plans have to go perfectly for us to share meaningful experiences, rather that we make the most of every opportunity to do so. We cannot wait for the ideal circumstances to be intentional; sometimes, you have to tell your friends to stop by even if your house is not in tip top shape and a meal is not prepared. These things are good but secondary. Though I am sure the disciples were happy to have those leftovers, this was hardly the highlight of their memory. It was being able to walk alongside Jesus and be apart of something amazing happening that made this time so special.

When we make time for quality time, we get to experience the amazing things happening in the lives of those we love. While we may not get to be there for everything, we will have new memories to share, stories to tell and bonds forged by our efforts to draw closer.

I think I may have a call or two to make. How about you?

CHAPTER 12:

"YOU KNOW I LOVE YOU, RIGHT?"

One of my favorite things in life is confrontation.

Okay, I am being factious. I think you would be hard-pressed to find anyone who would convey this sentiment, but I don't want to rule out that these people exist. Regardless, confrontation is an unavoidable aspect of life – my advice to those who try to actively avoid it is to quit while you're ahead.

As a pastor, confrontation is simply something that comes with the territory. In fact, when God wrote the job description, he made sure to highlight this (2 Timothy 3:16-4:2). From observing those who have pastored for years, it seems one gets better with experience. A former pastor of mine, in particular, had a way with this.

In times where he was engaged in even a mildly difficult conversation, I would often hear him say, "You know I love you, right?" What he did by saying this was reiterate his care for the individual(s). Though he needed to say something that would probably not be easy to hear, he made his motive clear; he was having the conversation as an expression of the love in his heart for them.

I suspect you have also had moments where you needed to lovingly bring something to someone's attention. The reasons for these moments vary but every relationship has them. While our friendships should not be a source of constant contention, they should also not be void of conflict. As

Proverbs 27:6 says, "Wounds from a friend can be trusted, but an enemy multiplies kisses."

Jesus was a great friend because he always told the truth, even at the risk of hurt feelings. He knew that walking in truth meant walking in freedom, and he wanted nothing less for those whom he loved. Some truths, although, are harder to receive than others. Furthermore, some people receive truth less readily than others. In Jesus' friend, Simon Peter, we see both at work.

Simon was one of those friends you absolutely love at times, and annoyingly fluster you in others. He was fiercely loyal but also inflexible. There were even occasions where he insisted he was right and Jesus was wrong. Here is a notable instance:

> [21] *From that time on Jesus began to explain to his disciples that he must go to Jerusalem and suffer many things at the hands of the elders, the chief priests and the teachers of the law, and that he must be killed and on the third day be raised to life.* [22] *Peter took him aside and began to rebuke him. "Never, Lord!" he said. "This shall never happen to you!"* [23] *Jesus turned and said to Peter, "Get behind me, Satan! You are a stumbling block to me; you do not have in mind the concerns of God, but merely human concerns."* (Matthew 16:21-23)

Sounds harsh, huh?

Yes, Jesus had to deliver some pretty sobering words to his friends at times, especially Peter. As we look as these moments, though, let us keep this in mind: love was his motive, truth was the method. Everything Jesus did was motivated by love. It is why he is not only the standard but foremost authority on the subject. Naturally, then, truth follows love, as its espousal is often an expression of concern and commitment. Love, truly, rejoices in the truth (1 Corinthians 13:6).

As we move on in our discussion, this is a good place to note what Jesus teaches us about this particular facet of friendship:

A call to friendship is a call to tell the truth.

What was the *truth* in this particular instance?

For starters, Jesus needed to convey to Peter *theological* truth. Peter not only had a faulty perspective concerning Jesus, but his fundamental understanding of Israel's Messiah was off target; he had just professed Jesus to be this person (Matthew 16:16). According to Simon, the Messiah was only a figure of triumph, not tragedy. The elders, chief priests and teachers of the law were supposed to be on the side of the Messiah, acknowledging him as king. Being "the Christ" was reserved for one who would have unparalleled military success, ridding God's people of his enemies. How could he be killed?

The Hebrew Scriptures are actually pretty clear about this. Isaiah the prophet, in particular, conveys how the King of kings is also the suffering servant:

> [11]*After he has suffered,*
>
> *he will see the light of life and be satisfied;*
>
> *by his knowledge my righteous servant will justify many,*
>
> *and he will bear their iniquities.*
>
> [12]*Therefore I will give him a portion among the great,*
>
> *and he will divide the spoils with the strong,*
>
> *because he poured out his life unto death,*
>
> *and was numbered with the transgressors.*
>
> *For he bore the sin of many,*
>
> *and made intercession for the transgressors.* (Isaiah 53:11-12)

Jesus was unwilling to allow Peter to continue in, essentially, his misunderstanding of the Scriptures. Whether Peter's messianic views were what he was led to believe or what he chose to believe, Jesus took the opportunity to insert truth into the exchange. Honestly, I would go as far as to say he had an obligation to do so; after all, he was a rabbi, called to correctly interpret God's truth.

We may not be rabbis (or Jewish for that matter), but we still have this same mandate. As God's people, we are not only committed to each other but also the truth of his Word. When someone espouses a belief that is incongruent with the Scripture, the onus is on us make the truth known—it does help to actually know it. This is not a responsibility to pass on to the seemingly "more qualified." If we are truly committed to our friends, we are committed to them walking in God's truth.

Concerning this, Paul writes the following:

> [14]*Then we will no longer be infants, tossed back and forth by the waves, and blown here and there by every wind of teaching and by the cunning and craftiness of people in their deceitful scheming.* [15]*Instead, speaking the truth in love, we will grow to become in every respect the mature body of him who is the head, that is, Christ.* (Ephesians 4:14-15)

In communicating this kind of truth, we keep our friends from harm. Peter's theology was one of a revolutionary. His belief in how the reign of God would be established on the earth would have led him down the wrong path, the war path. Bearing arms and trying to take over the world by force would not only have proved unsuccessful but fatal. Most dangerously, this was a path that opposed God.

This is not a license for us to go on a theological rampage, instead being an opportunity to bear witness to the truth of God's Word. In doing so, we can help our friends realign their perspective with God's. As David so aptly says of the Scriptures, "By them your servant is warned; in keeping them there is great reward" (Psalm 19:11).

Secondly, Jesus needed to convey to Peter *objective* truth. Having challenged Simon's theology concerning messianic prophesy, Jesus simply stated the plain fact of the matter: he was not thinking straight on the subject.

There are times where we have to make this same assertion to our own friends. We all can be taken captive by our own thoughts and feelings on occasion. The truth from a friend is often the key that opens the door to sobriety and sincerity. Proverbs 28:26 says, "Whoever trusts in his own mind is a fool, but he who walks in wisdom will be delivered" (ESV).

Objectivity is one of the greatest gifts we can give to our friends. It is these moments of honesty that help to shape and sharpen us, being equipped with greater insight for our journey. I have received this "gift" quite a few times. Admittedly, I have not always been the most grateful recipient, but my journey would be much different without it.

At the church where I currently serve as an associate pastor, I am also privileged to lead the music ministry. Music has always been a passion of mine. I started singing when I was 10 years old – it was actually kind of an accident. My cousins were leaving for a choir rehearsal at the church my family was attending in Detroit, while I had no plans on going. For fear of being left out, I decided to tag along.

After some time of singing in the choir, people around me noticed I actually had a pretty nice voice. I spent my teen years cultivating this craft at my church, school and in a community group. It felt good to be good at something, and the people around me were always complimentary.

When I came to Chicago, my musical pursuits continued. This led me to audition for the worship team at my former church. From the excellence I observed from the pews, I knew this was a serious group of singers; I considered it a privilege to join the team. Having served in the ministry for a while, the opportunity eventually presented itself for me to lead a song. After a few times rehearsing it, though, things did not seem to be going well.

In an effort to be supportive, my teammates did not call a spade a spade; if they were not going to say anything, neither was I.

The worship leader on staff at the church did not take the same stance. Yes, it was her job to ensure our ministry of music was edifying (which means it had to sound good) but she was arguably even more committed to seeing us become all God wanted. In the most loving way, she told me I was not ready to lead congregational worship at our church. It was hard to hear but very much necessary. I had been singing for years, yet I still somehow needed to find my voice, and the conviction necessary to lead people in this way.

Her saying this to me was, ironically, the catalyst which began my ministry of worship leading. I was not ready but I was determined to become ready – I even ended up singing the song after all. To this day, I consider her a great friend; she has always been a person in my life I can go to for the truth.

We need people in our lives who will shoot it to us straight. The desire for us to hear what we want to hear, and the pressure we can apply to people for this response, make it even more necessary. If this did not happen in my life, I would certainly not be anyone's worship leader. Think of the opportunities we can forfeit if we do not heed this kind of truth, as well as the opportunities our friends will miss if we withhold.

Jesus, also, had to convey to Peter *relational* truth. He did not have a correct understanding of the nature of the Messiah, making him dead wrong in his thinking and approach. This, though, was a stumbling block to Jesus. While Simon may have thought he was helping, he was actually hurting, and Jesus made this plain to him.

You may be asking, "Did Peter really deserve to be called *Satan?*"

Well, desperate times often call for desperate measures.

Jesus was moving closer to the events he predicted, and the person who was to be the leader of the group had the absolute wrong impression of things. This was so the case that Peter actually refuted the fundamental aspects of Christianity, the death and resurrection of its Christ. Simon was setting himself in opposition against Jesus. It is no wonder, then, why he calls him "Satan," as the name literally means *adversary.*

If Peter (or any of the disciples) was going to continue to follow Jesus, it could not be under false pretenses or with selfish motives. No, Peter had to realize that self-sacrifice was the way of God's kingdom; this not only meant coming to terms with Jesus' death but also being willing to die for him. Jesus continues:

> [24]*Then Jesus said to his disciples, "Whoever wants to be my disciple must deny themselves and take up their cross and follow me.* [25]*For whoever wants to save their life will lose it, but whoever loses their life for me will find it.* (Matthew 16:24-25)

This moment was pivotal in their relationship. While Jesus could have avoided or even disowned Simon, he decided to choose the forward path, which was one of relational truth. Sometimes, we have moments in our friendships where a friend's behavior is negatively impacting us. In conveying this we are able to not only make a loving appeal but also promote change.

In college, there was a time when I was really difficult to be around. For some reason (honestly, I don't even remember), I found myself in a funk; things did not taste the same, the world lost its color and nothing seemed fun. I was noticeably unhappy, and this started to impact my friends. My disposition was dampening our every interaction, and my communication ceased to be life-giving.

One night, I had a pivotal conversation with my then roommate. We were not super close at the time but we had the same group of friends and an appreciation for one another. His words to me expressed a deep sense of commitment and were also the catalyst for my behavioral turnaround. What he said was not super revelatory – essentially, I just needed to get my act together. That he was willing to say something opened my eyes to the commitment I was not expressing to our shared friends. It also opened the door for my roommate and I to become close friends as a result.

There have been times where I have simply had to face the music, especially after having done a disservice to someone with my words or actions. From things such as communicating in frustration to leaving promises unfulfilled, people have lovingly decided to take the forward path with me by sharing the truth. Honestly, not only are those relationships stronger but I am all the better for it.

As friends, we are to be messengers of truth to each other. After all, if we are not, who else will?

CHAPTER 13:

"LOYALTY"

Few things are more admirable in life than a loyal friend.

When someone is at your side through thick-and-thin, having your back when you need them, you truly do not want to let them go. While you may assume everyone has this type of person in their life, loyalty is not as common as you may think. Some may have experienced empty promises of help from people on whom they were truly dependent. Others possibly had friendships dissolve because of competition, professionally or even personally. As the writer of Proverbs says, "Many will say they are loyal friends, but who can find one who is truly reliable?" (Proverbs 20:6 NLT).

Yes, loyalty is quite the commodity. It is something, however, we should find in our friendships, namely because we are demonstrating it. When it comes to this demonstration, Jesus provides us with the best example.

7Finally, he said to his disciples, "Let's go back to Judea."

8But his disciples objected. "Rabbi," they said, "only a few days ago the people in Judea were trying to stone you. Are you going there again?"

11Then he said, "Our friend Lazarus has fallen asleep, but now I will go and wake him up."

¹²The disciples said, "Lord, if he is sleeping, he will soon get better!" ¹³They thought Jesus meant Lazarus was simply sleeping, but Jesus meant Lazarus had died.

¹⁴So he told them plainly, "Lazarus is dead. ¹⁵And for your sakes, I'm glad I wasn't there, for now you will really believe. Come, let's go see him."

¹⁶Thomas, nicknamed the Twin, said to his fellow disciples, "Let's go, too—and die with Jesus." (John 11:7-8, 11-16 NLT)

So far, we have considered Jesus' relationship with the group of friends affectionately known as the 12 disciples. Certainly, Jesus spent the most time with them during the three years he ministered. From the above passage, though, it is clear the Twelve were not his *only* friends. We are introduced to another: Lazarus.

Lazarus was the brother of probably the two most famous sisters in the Bible, Mary and Martha. They lived together in Bethany, which was only two miles from Jerusalem. The gospels detail at least two occasions where Jesus stayed with the family (Luke 10:38-39; John 12:1-3) and intimate some others (Matthew 21:17; Mark 11:11, 19). Seeing that they lived so close to Jerusalem, it is likely he visited them at least three times a year (Deuteronomy 16:16).

We may not know much else about Lazarus but we do know Jesus considered him a friend. In fact, Mary and Martha relayed the news of Lazarus' condition to Jesus by saying, "Lord, the one you love is sick" (John 11:3). Maybe this is a lesson for us in itself. Friendship is truly based on the love we have for someone, and this love stands on its own.

Jesus loved him so much, he was willing to make a return trip to Judea. This is noteworthy for two reasons. First, Bethany was at least a 20-mile walk from Jesus' nearest suspected location, which included crossing the Jordan River. I can't say I have ever traveled eight hours to visit a friend, not even one who was sick.

Secondly, and most importantly, Jesus' previous trip to Judea was not the greatest experience. After making public his claim of being God, he and his disciples had to escape for their lives after some Jews threatened to stone them. This is, actually, quite an *amazing* paradox. Jesus was confident enough in his divinity to make this declaration to the Jews during one of their annual feasts but certain enough of his humanity to recognize his mortality. Needless to say, the people in Judea had a bone to pick with him, and they were willing to kill him over it.

Jesus, however, would indeed make this return trip. It may have been inconvenient, it may have been dangerous, but this was not going to stop him from being there for a friend in need. To be sure, it is not that those things were dismissed; after all, they left Judea for a reason. For Jesus, inconvenience and personal cost could not outweigh the value of friendship – this is loyalty at its finest.

As a result of this gesture, his disciples made the return trip with him. They would, of course, experience the same inconvenience and the same threat of danger but chose to put these things to the side to be there for both Lazarus and Jesus. Thomas, knowing death is a possible consequence for following Jesus back to Judea, says "let us also go." He demonstrated a loyalty that truly runs deep, and so did the other disciples.

My friends, let us not forget this all-important lesson that Jesus teaches us:

We foster mutual loyalty in our friendships when we ourselves are loyal.

When Jesus said, "Do to others as you would have them do to you" (Luke 6:31), he did not have friendship in view. On the contrary, he was talking about how to love our enemies. While we are to practice this with people who do not have the best of intentions toward us, this does seem like something to also carry over into our closest relationships. After all, isn't this how Jesus lived?

It goes without saying that Jesus was committed to the disciples. He chose them, taught them, confided in them and even washed their dirty feet (John 13:5). His display of loyalty toward Lazarus, a man we do not even hear about outside of John's gospel, may even provide a keener picture of his devotion.

Jesus and Lazarus certainly did not spend every day together, as was the case with Jesus and the Twelve. In fact, they probably did not see each other unless Jesus made his way to Bethany; this is possibly why only the apostle John mentions him. Lazarus is perhaps like the friend who always invites you to their place to hang out but seldom comes to yours. Yet, it was he for whom Jesus was willing to put his neck on the line. This so inspiring that the disciples could not help but follow suit.

Loyalty may be hard to find but it is also contagious. As a person expresses their devotion toward others, this fosters an environment of devotion, where people genuinely desire to remain steadfast in their commitment. If you have had a friend like this, you know what I mean.

When I think of those in my life I call friends, I consider myself truly blessed. My wife and I often joke about how the word "friend" is defined – more aptly, how I define it – and who makes it into this category. For me, it is much more about the quality of these people than the quantity. One such person is my good friend, Robert.

Robert is genuinely one of the nicest people you will ever meet. At the time of writing, my pastor actually mentions him by name in a sermon, commenting on how nice he is as a person. More than the topic of discussion in the pulpit, though, Robert is the real deal. He is always there for you when you need him and is there with a smile on his face.

As Heidi and I were preparing for marriage, the time came for her things to be moved into the place where we would be living; needless to say, she had a lot more things than I did. Of course, as her fiancé, my presence during the move was all but assumed, even fundamentally required. Don't get me wrong, I love my wife more than anyone or anything but Jesus.

However, it's also a fact that I hate moving. Personally, when I help someone else move, I am displaying the grandest of loving gestures.

I know everyone may not feel as strongly but my suspicion is that moving is hardly making anyone's top ten list of favorite things to do. While I was not sure who would be there to help, I had no doubts about Robert. Sure enough, he was one of the first ones to arrive and last to leave. When I look back at that day, as much as I dislike moving, I remember it fondly, because of the people who were there for us when we needed them, people like Robert.

Truly the "Roberts" in our friend groups make it difficult to not return the favor. This is not a matter of guilt but of the space these people occupy in our hearts. When the time came for Robert and his family to move into their new home, the response of people who were willing to come lay new flooring, paint walls and just be of service could not have been more telling of the life of loyalty he lives. If my friend's life is any indicator, Proverbs is proven right when it says, "A generous person will prosper; whoever refreshes others will be refreshed" (11:25).

Generally speaking, there are times when rules have exceptions. There may be a situation where you show loyalty to someone and it is not recip-rocated (more on this in the next chapter). Our motive for loyalty, though, is not the response of others; we are loyal because of the example of Christ. His amazing life is what inspires us and gives us hope for how others will respond. Jesus' own words anchor this hope, when he says the following:

> Give, and it will be given to you. A good measure, pressed down, shaken together and running over, will be poured into your lap. For with the measure you use, it will be measured to you. (Luke 6:38)

Let us, then, give an abundant measure of loyalty to our friends; when we do so, it truly will be given in return. It might not be convenient and may require sacrifice but it is always worthwhile. I can only imagine the joys

Lazarus' friends and family experienced at his resurrection. Even more, I can only imagine the awe of the disciples realizing Jesus is the "resurrection and the life" (John 11:25). This is the message to which Jesus' disciples have remained loyal ever since.

CHAPTER 14:

"FORGIVENESS"

Jesus' friends were certainly with him during some tough times, but they were not *always* loyal.

Despite his unyielding faithfulness to those whom he loved, even he had moments where he was let down; talk about an exception to a rule. While loyalty is the way to live, it does not guarantee reciprocity, though it does promote it. The interesting thing about people is that they will always be people; nobody does anything perfectly, especially when it comes to relationships.

Each of us has limits, things which challenge our preconceived notions of self and of our commitment to others. We discover these limits at different junctures in our lives, as we journey through life's changing seasons. For the disciples, they encountered theirs at perhaps the most inopportune time – this was at least the case for Jesus.

The hour had finally come for Jesus to make his way to the cross. He had been trying to prepare the Twelve for this moment, even foretelling his death on three occasions according to the synoptic gospel writers. They had been with him when he was almost stoned in Judea, when the winds and waves were raging on the Sea of Galilee (Mark 4:35-41) and for the mass exodus of followers after the 5,000 were fed (John 6:66-68). If anyone was faithful to Jesus, it was these guys. They, then, certainly had cause to believe this would not change.

On the night of his arrest, Jesus made some remarks to the disciples that were probably painful, for both him and them. This is made clearer by the disciples' response, namely Peter. Here is the conversation:

> [31] *Then Jesus told them, "This very night you will all fall away on account of me, for it is written:*
>
> *"'I will strike the shepherd,*
>
> *and the sheep of the flock will be scattered.'*
>
> [32] *But after I have risen, I will go ahead of you into Galilee."*
>
> [33] *Peter replied, "Even if all fall away on account of you, I never will."*
>
> [34] *"Truly I tell you," Jesus answered, "this very night, before the rooster crows, you will disown me three times."*
>
> [35] *But Peter declared, "Even if I have to die with you, I will never disown you." And all the other disciples said the same.*
> (Matthew 26:31-35)

Despite the loyalty the disciples had displayed thus far, Jesus tells them they have officially reached their limit. It would seem they had enough to draw from to endure this moment but the pressure was just too great; subsequently, Jesus even prayed three times for the Father to take this bitter cup from him (Matthew 26:36-44). Not only was he certain of his disciples' defection, he even had Scripture to support his claim. If someone is going to burn you, perhaps it is helpful to know in advance.

None of the Twelve were willing to concede this, and certainly not Peter. He may have been wrong about Jesus dying, so much so that he was corrected in front of the others, but he would not be mistaken about his own commitment. Peter, in defending himself, goes to such lengths that he slightly throws the others under the bus – the pressure of a moment sometimes causes us to stop caring for others and worry about ourselves. The other disciples seem to overlook this slight, in an effort to assure Jesus of their unyielding fidelity.

Honestly, it would have been hard for anyone in the disciples' shoes to receive Jesus' words. When the person you leave everything to follow for three years suddenly says you will desert him this very night, it is both shocking and offensive. He had said things previously which were tough pills to swallow but this was in a category of its own (maybe right up there with being called, "Satan"). As we have established, though, something being difficult to hear does not make it any less true.

After Jesus and the disciples spend time in prayer, the temple soldiers arrive at Gethsemane to arrest him. Famously, Judas, one of the Twelve, identifies Jesus for the arresting officers. Jesus had predicted his betrayal (Matthew 26:20-25) but I am sure it was still painful. Matthew, who was present for the events he recounts, pours more salt in the wound when he gives his final commentary on this scene:

Then all the disciples deserted him and fled. (Matthew 26:56b)

While the relationship between Jesus and the disciples is at this point in critical condition, there is still one transgression left to occur. Peter, perhaps Jesus' most loyal friend, was to deny him – not just once but three times in the same night. Can you imagine your best friend going around and telling people he does not know you? Jesus found himself alone, and his "friends" certainly were not acting like it.

My friend, I know that you are no stranger to pain. People you love have let you down by saying hurtful things, betraying your confidence or not being there when you needed them. While being hurt is no crime, if not careful, we can carry these feelings for years, siphoning precious time and energy from ourselves and our relationships. How, then, do we respond to offense from those whom we least expect it? How did Jesus?

It actually was helpful for Jesus to know about the disciples' failings in advance. When he experienced these moments, his world did not crumble. On the contrary, he had a perspective that accounted for these occasions of disappointment. Though it seems we do not have this same advantage, Jesus actually gives us a great degree of foresight in sharing the following words with the disciples: "It is impossible that no offenses should come" (Luke 17:1a NKJV).

In Christ's words, we may not find the specifics of how this will happen from friend to friend but we do have a general assurance that it is *impossible* to avoid offense. Yes, eventually, even those closest to us will wrong us. This is not always a capital crime but can be a relational misdemeanor; we have laws in our hearts and minds, perhaps unknown to our friends and ourselves, which seem to be easily broken. Coming to terms with the reality of offense is our first step in not being crippled by it.

When we come to this realization, we are armed with the resolve to look beyond these moments. Amidst the discussion about the disciples' defection and denial, Jesus says to them, "after I have risen, I will go ahead of you into Galilee." It becomes clear that Jesus did not initiate this conversation to find fault; he was simply being honest. Jesus was not determined to hold a grudge. In fact, he was looking forward to the day when these events would be behind them.

What Jesus teaches us is this:

In order for our friendships to last, we must forgive.

After abandoning Jesus when he needed them most, the disciples likely felt a deep sense of shame. Add to that the guilt of his death at the hands of the Roman authorities and you will see why they may have forgotten the "good part" of their conversation with him. For starters, Jesus said he would rise from the dead, which he mentioned on multiple occasions. Secondly, he would not only meet them in Galilee but was going *ahead* of them. Yes, it was Jesus who took the initiative to restore their friendship, even after they deserted him.

It may not seem fair, but forgiveness often places the onus on the offended to make the first move. Jesus speaks to this when he says, "If another believer sins against you, go privately and point out the offense" (Matthew 18:15a NLT). While all the disciples should have showed up at the tomb on Sunday morning, it was Jesus who journeyed from his burial site outside of Jerusalem to seek them. Similarly, there are times when we have to initiate the conversation. In doing so, we set the stage for repentance and reconciliation.

Two names you may have never heard, Mary Johnson and Oshea Israel, provide a most profound example of this. In 1993, a then 16-year-old Oshea attended a party where Mary's 20-year-old son, Laramiun, was also present. After getting into an argument, Oshea shot and killed Laramiun – he was Mary's only son.

About 11 years later, Mary reached out to her son's killer to ask if the two of them could meet. After her initial request was declined, she waited another nine months to ask again. It seemed such a senseless killing to her, and she needed the closure of knowing why her son was taken from her at such a young age. Mary's second request to visit Oshea was granted.

Upon meeting, Mary realized this was not the same 16-year-old who she had seen in the courtroom all those years ago; she recalled wanting to do harm to him. Their time together instead began with a handshake and ended with a hug. They spent two hours simply getting to know each other, and as Mary talked about Laramiun, he became "more human" to Oshea. At the end of their meeting, Mary was so overcome by emotion that Oshea had to hold her up to keep her from falling. She reflected on this moment after he left the room, saying, "I just hugged the man who murdered my son."

In a later interview with Oshea, now released from prison, Mary commented, "I instantly knew that all that anger and the animosity, all the stuff I had in my heart for 12 years for you — I knew it was over, that I had totally forgiven you." [22] [23] Today, not only are the two next door neighbors but their relationship is very much that of a mother and son.

Forgiveness, even on the deepest of levels, is possible for all of us. Not only are our relationships sustained by forgiveness but it provides a clean canvas. What was once sullied by disunity can now be used to create new intimacy, new understanding and new growth. Our friendships may even feel brand new – this was certainly the case for Mary and Oshea.

As for the disciples, Jesus wanted to have a relationship with them on new terms. The very covenant he came to enact with God's people, the New Covenant, accounted for their sins and made provision for their forgiveness; this is the same covenant he commemorated with his disciples at supper, on the night of his arrest. It would, officially, take effect when Jesus rose from the dead.

In Matthew's gospel, when Jesus appears to his disciples after emerging from his tomb, he does not take the opportunity to have an "I told you so" moment. No, he was not as concerned about the past as he was the future. He had come to wade the waters of sin and these imperfect men were chosen to be closest to him. When it comes to forgiveness, his silence on what had transpired just days prior is perhaps the most powerful illustration he gives:

> [18]*Then Jesus came to them and said, "All authority in heaven and on earth has been given to me. [19]Therefore go and make disciples of all nations, baptizing them in the name of the Father and of the Son and of the Holy Spirit, [20]and teaching them to obey everything I have commanded you. And surely I am with you always, to the very end of the age."* (Matthew 28:18-20)

Is there a friend you need to forgive?

---

22   NPR. (2011, May 20). Forgiving Her Son's Killer: 'Not an Easy Thing'. Retrieved July 21, 2020, from https://www.npr.org/2011/05/20/136463363/forgiving-her-sons-killer-not-an-easy-thing

23   Isay, D. (2013, October 23). You killed my son...and I forgive you. Retrieved July 21, 2020, from https://www.thedailybeast.com/you-killed-my-sonand-i-forgive-you

Could there be an offense you have been holding against someone you love?

Forgiveness can be difficult but it is possible. When we extend this to each other, our relationships become stronger, more enduring and also the catalyst for fruitfulness and blessing to others.

Jesus is with us always, and he wants us to demonstrate the same lasting commitment to our friends.

CHAPTER 15:

"LOVE"

By now, it has probably become clear that friendships are deeply dependent on one thing: love.

Love is what motivates us to make time for someone, tell them a difficult truth, remain loyal and, of course, extend forgiveness; it truly does cover a multitude of sins (1 Peter 4:8). Our relationships not only thrive because of this deep affection but they would prove quite difficult to maintain without it. This is what made Jesus such a great friend. He demonstrated a love that was, honestly, unprecedented. He was always giving, ultimately offering his very life.

We, now, turn our attention to the passage which opened this section:

12My command is this: Love each other as I have loved you. 13Greater love has no one than this: to lay down one's life for one's friends. 14You are my friends if you do what I command. 15I no longer call you servants, because a servant does not know his master's business. Instead, I have called you friends, for every-thing that I learned from my Father I have made known to you. (John 15:12-15)

Jesus, as to be expected, sets an incredibly high standard. The disciples had grown up hearing the famous words, "Love your neighbor as yourself"

(Leviticus 19:18), in addition to Jesus repeating them during his three years of ministry (Matthew 22:39, Mark 12:31). While this command was already lofty, the rest of the law was often used to dilute the true intentions of these words. In light of Jesus instituting a new covenant, he issues a new command: "Love each other…*as I have loved you.*"

To Jesus friendship does not mean reciprocity - simply treating the people in your life the way they treat you. Friendship, instead, is a constant pursuit of the best interests of those you love, even at your own expense. When quality time is not being pursued by our friends, love is what makes us pick up the phone. If the truth is being withheld by a friend, love causes our commitment to truth to not waver. Loyalty and forgiveness are not limited to mutuality in the presence of love; they are, rather, a constant pouring from a generous heart.

It was this kind of love that Jesus was requiring of his friends. The emphasis is not how they treated him, however, but how they would treat *one another*. Yes, they did let him down on the night of his arrest, but they had given everything to follow him. Jesus had seen people come and go but the disciples stayed with him; all the while, his own family did not believe in him. When the notion of their defection is mentioned, they clamored to insist this would not be the case.

The interactions they had with each other give reason for why Jesus stresses this love amongst themselves. On multiple occasions, they argued about who would be the greatest in the kingdom (Luke 9:46; 22:24); James and John actually resorted to using their mother in a ploy to jockey for position (Matthew 20:20-24). At the Last Supper, it was clear the disciples were not yet committed to serving one another, as Jesus goes to the length of washing feet in an effort to instill this in their hearts (John 13:1-17). Loving Jesus was easy, it was loving each other that would require work. Jesus, in light of this, was leaving the most powerful motive for this love: his example.

As you consider this topic of love, you may find yourself asking, "Why didn't we discuss this sooner?" Having walked through Jesus' life as a son and brother, these certainly seem appropriate places for this to be mentioned.

Again, Jesus is love personified; you cannot talk about any aspect of his life and not run into love. While there have been traces throughout, we are focusing on love at this point for a couple of reasons. For starters, the principles of friendship can be applied to really any relationship. Can you think of one relationship of note in your life that does not need quality time, truthful speech, loyalty and forgiveness?

Secondly, while we are born into our families, our friends are the people in our lives that we have chosen. The notion of choosing someone to be a part of your life amplifies the concept of love. Yes, we should love our families. There is, however, an innate desire to do so; at worst, there is an innate sense of duty to do so. Saying to someone that you have made a choice to commit to them, having no other obligation but that of love, speaks most loudly. This, it seems, is why Jesus says, "You did not choose me, but I chose you" (John 15:16a).

Jesus' selection made these twelve men the most privileged of people. They had a front row seat to the greatest demonstration of love ever known. Walking with him every day for three years, the disciples not only saw how Jesus' heart went out to complete strangers but they themselves experienced his patient care and affection. In the conversation John recounts, Jesus alludes to the pinnacle of this expression: the giving of his very life. Writing his first epistle, John exhorts followers of Jesus to emulate this kind of love:

> *We know what real love is because Jesus gave up his life for us. So we also ought to give up our lives for our brothers and sisters.* (1 John 3:16 NLT)

When it comes to friendship, or any relationship, there is truly nothing greater than this sacrificial kind of love. A person possessed by this love is willing to give of themselves in a way that inspires even the most reluctant to do the same. Jesus giving in this way for his friends teaches us a most powerful lesson:

"Friendships" are only such if we are
willing to lay it all on the line.

Perhaps friendship does not mean what it once did. The social media age, while making connection accessible in unprecedented ways, has in large part achieved this more broadly, not more deeply. One can have hundreds, even thousands, of "friends" with no real sense of commitment. Says historian Henry Adams, "One friend in a lifetime is much; two are many; three are hardly possible."[24] It is, of course, within reason to have three or more friends. The sentiment does not have to do as much with the number as much as it does what each relationship requires.

Though many of us draw a distinction between our platforms and our personal lives, one cannot help but be affected by this notion of convenience in relationships. Having things on our terms is always easiest. This is why I am more apt to wish someone a "happy birthday" with a quick comment rather than what could be a lengthy call. Friendship, however, is not meant to be convenient, rather the giving of oneself for the benefit of another person.

Recounting the last serveral years of my life, there have been people who were really good to me, much more than I deserved. These acts of kindness cannot be attributed to anything other than the example of Christ. One such time involved a really good friend of mine, Michael Moore (no, not the filmmaker).

Mike and I served together at a college campus church plant where he was the pastor. This was a really special season in my life. I felt a call to the ministry, and serving these college students under Mike's leadership was a wonderful opportunity to learn and grow. He was always vocal about how much he appreciated me coming in after my full-time job to volunteer but it was truly my life being enriched by both he and these special young

---

24   *The Education of Henry Adams, ch. 20 (1907)*

people. After having been apart of the church for a while, Mike decided he wanted to show his gratitude more tangibly, mailing me a check for $1,000.

For anyone, this would be an incredibly generous gesture but especially for him. Mike's livelyhood was the support he raised for his ministry on campus; as you can probably imagine, this was a modest amount. There was no retirement or 401k for someone in his position, and meeting the next year's budget needs was always a step of faith. Yes, Mike is certainly a prudent man financially but this was sacrificial giving at its best. I was able to purchase my first car because of Mike's generosity, an act of love I will remember for the rest of my life.

Many of us will not find ourselves in a position to, literally, give our lives for the sake of another. We are able, however, to give of our time, energy and resources. This is why John expounds on his exhortation to love as Christ did:

> [16]*We know what real love is because Jesus gave up his life for us. So we also ought to give up our lives for our brothers and sisters.* [17]*If someone has enough money to live well and sees a brother or sister in need but shows no compassion—how can God's love be in that person?* [18]*Dear children, let's not merely say that we love each other; let us show the truth by our actions.*
> (1 John 3:16-18 NLT)

Love calls us to action, not a response. It does not wait for someone else to make the first move. On the contrary, love even prompts us to go to those who may not comprehend it or who may not be ready to receive it. Is not this what Jesus did with the disciples? With each of us?

While love certainly does not qualify, it does have qualities. As Jesus shares with his disciples on the night of his arrest, he alludes to one of them. He says that they are no longer servants but friends, because he has divulged everything he had learned from the Father. The disciples were privy to things others were not – what a fitting thing to say about one's friends. They had plenty of shared experiences but friendship was about something more to Jesus: he needed to be able to trust them with the things that mattered most. Love does a lot of things but it is not its truest unless it "trusts" (1 Corinthians 13:7).

Trust in any relationship is vitally important. For Jesus, this is what separated those who merely followed from those who were truly friends. Indeed, he gave his life for the entire world, providing the most powerful example of love. He, though, only reveals his secrets to those closest to him. Loving our friends looks a lot like being vulnerable.

Can we truly say we are loving if we are not giving?

Moreover, can we truly say we are giving if we are not pouring from the inner most places of our hearts?

This is what it means to be a great friend. This is what it means to be like Jesus.

SECTION FOUR:

"AN AMAZING HUSBAND" – JESUS THE HUSBAND

Ephesians 5:25

> *Husbands, love your wives, just as Christ loved the church and*
> *gave himself up for her*

While Jesus is the example for all of us to follow, it cannot be overlooked that he was, indeed, a man.

Our journey thus far has largely explored aspects of Christ's life that are seamlessly applicable, regardless of gender. His identity as a male, nonetheless, means there are ways he relates specifically to men. God's original design called for men to be leaders. This leadership is foremost expressed in the role of husband.

As men, our role as husbands is our chief responsibility. We are to provide for, protect and pastor the one entrusted to our care – all this being an expression of an unquenchable love. Jesus, while he did not have a traditional wedding, remains the example for every husband as the bridegroom of the church (Matthew 9:15; Revelation 19:7). In fact, his is the only marriage which will last for all eternity.

Jesus shows us that effectively leading as husbands is not only a barometer for how we are running but also our wives. The gospels offer a snapshot of Jesus' husbandly nature, namely through his interactions with different women. While these interactions were numerous, we will focus on an at-length encounter with a certain Samaritan woman in John chapter 4.

The Samaritan Woman – John 4:1-30

At some point in time, I am sure we all have talked with a friend or loved one about who they would eventually marry.

Whether this meant running down a list of traits or naming an actual person, we must concede that the accuracy of these conversations is in large part pretty low. Even for myself, I said on numerous occasions, "I will never date anyone that I work with." Not only did I break this rule but my wife and I are staff members at the same church. I must admit, I have never been happier to be wrong.

In Jesus' day it would probably not be strange for a Jewish man to have a list of some sort. It likely included things like having a good reputation, never having been married and being in good health. Interestingly enough, Jesus found himself in the company of women who were prostitutes, widows and had debilitating illnesses. Even still, there is one thing that would have united the lists of every Jewish man: she could not be a Samaritan.

The storied past between the Jews and Samaritans brought them to a relational impasse. As a Jewish person, if you were traveling from Judea to Galilee you would take the longer route just to avoid Samaria, which was conveniently situated between the two. Even when Jesus and his disciples tried to pass through Samaria to get to Jerusalem, they rejected him; this prompted James and John to suggest they call fire from heaven to destroy them (Luke 9:51-55). In the words of John, "Jews do not associate with Samaritans" (John 4:9b).

This time, though, Jesus "had to go through Samaria" (John 4:4). Yes, he was tired from the journey; going the shorter route would have certainly been beneficial. John, however, clarifies that this detour was for the sole purpose of meeting a woman at a well.

CHAPTER 16:

"INITIATING" (V. 1-8)

¹Now Jesus learned that the Pharisees had heard that he was gaining and baptizing more disciples than John— ²although in fact it was not Jesus who baptized, but his disciples. ³So he left Judea and went back once more to Galilee.

⁴Now he had to go through Samaria. ⁵So he came to a town in Samaria called Sychar, near the plot of ground Jacob had given to his son Joseph. ⁶Jacob's well was there, and Jesus, tired as he was from the journey, sat down by the well. It was about noon.

⁷When a Samaritan woman came to draw water, Jesus said to her, "Will you give me a drink?" ⁸(His disciples had gone into the town to buy food.)

Jesus knew something that every man has learned, sometimes from personal experience: it is difficult to talk to a girl with an audience.

Having started yet another trip home to Galilee, his decision to cut through Samaria leads him to a well in a town called Sychar. That it was noon when Jesus arrived is no small detail. You see, people did not typically go to wells to draw water at this time of day, because of the intense heat from the sun. Instead, they would do so toward the end of the day. Jesus knew this woman would be alone; this was, in fact, her intention. As such,

Jesus allows his disciples to take a field trip into town while he remained at the well.

Even with no audience, I have found it challenging in these instances to know what to say. In fact, for the moments I remember asking someone out, I had rehearsed ahead of time – if I was given the opportunity, I certainly did not want to blow it! Prior to asking out Heidi, I even prayed for the right moment (no audience) and the right words to say. Interestingly enough, Jesus' first words to this unnamed woman were, "Will you give me a drink?"

As the ensuing conversation will reveal, these words carried much more meaning than meets the eye. Jesus was very purposeful in their selection, and they spoke to his desired end. Nothing about this exchange was incidental but it was planned from the moment he headed north for Galilee. Knowing this woman's itinerary was not enough. If he wanted to talk with her, he would need to initiate.

Being the standard bearer for husbands everywhere, the first lesson we glean from Jesus' exchange with the Samaritan woman is this:

As husbands, we are to initiate with our wives.

Intuitively, this is something we all know and have probably practiced. After all, the reason we are married in the first place is because of this pursuit. Proverbs 18:22 wisely says, "He who finds a wife finds what is good and receives favor from the Lord." That a wife needs to be found means the man has to do the searching. This initiation, though, is not something that ends at the marriage altar. In fact, we should find ourselves initiating for the rest of our lives.

While dating, initiating can seem more adventurous. The sheer thrill of the chase fosters in a man a creativity that can even leave himself surprised. Planning these outings is effortless when you are not thinking about bills, children and keeping a home in order. After starting your lives together, initiation takes on a different tone. Marriage experts, Drs. Les and Leslie Parrott, share from their experience on this topic:

> Recognizing how fundamentally different men and women are allowed me (Leslie) to see that Les courted me to get married. It's that simple. Once we married, his purpose of courtship was accomplished, and he was ready to move on to other productive activities. It turned out that his "sweet nothings" were not "nothings" after all, but whisperings calculated to persuade me to the altar.[25]

Many of us can relate to Les. In our minds, it makes sense that upon marriage we will simply not pursue as we did prior; after all, we have already established a lasting commitment. It is not that we love our wives any less but to us this season of life requires something different. Yes, this love will evolve over time but the thread of initiation should remain.

The need for our wives to be valued, esteemed and delighted in deserves our regular attention. Understandably, you would not want to have to consistently remind someone of your relational needs. As husbands, then, this means we have to be proactive; we have to initiate. In many cases, this will be premeditated, just as Jesus planned his arrival to Jacob's well for this fateful conversation with the Samaritan woman. There will be times, still, where you are prompted in a given moment to initiate a loving exchange or spontaneous endeavor.

Sure, with children, doing things in the "spur of the moment" is not as easy. If you want to take your wife out on a date, you have to find a babysitter. Even for those of us who are most networked, this can at times be difficult. While we do need to take our wives out on a date, this is not the only impromptu gesture we can make.

---

25   Parrott, L., & Parrott, L. (2015). Question Five: Have You Bridged the Gender Gap? In *Saving your marriage before it starts* (p. 118). Grand Rapids, MI: Zondervan.

Just the other day, when thinking of how to apply this in my own life, I happened to stop at the grocery store on my way home from the office. Though I was going for the purpose of getting potatoes, I saw an opportunity to initiate. I didn't have time for what I would consider the grandest of gestures – those potatoes were needed for that night's dinner! What I did have time for was to do something meaningful. When I arrived home, I not only had in tow the potatoes we needed but also a bouquet of roses. Suffice it to say, they were very much appreciated.

The struggle for us, at times, is not seeing the utility in doing something. It is in our hearts to initiate but we are juggling so many things that we have to quantify our decisions, especially concerning time and money. What we need to perceive is that initiating does have an inherent utility: meeting the relational need of our partner. This is hard to quantify, as it is truly invaluable.

The concept of initiating intimates a flare for the romantic but does include other things as well. In our marriages, we have financial matters to resolve, vacations to be planned and decisions to be made, all of which require someone to start the discussion. This does not always have to be the husband's role but should be the norm.

The form of initiation truest to the text, though, is conversations that are difficult. While this is seldom fun for anyone, every relationship of note will require one of these at some point in time. What matters is how these conversations are navigated.

CHAPTER 17:

"EXPOSING THE REAL ISSUE" (V. 9-15)

⁹The Samaritan woman said to him, "You are a Jew and I am a Samaritan woman. How can you ask me for a drink?" (For Jews do not associate with Samaritans.)

¹⁰Jesus answered her, "If you knew the gift of God and who it is that asks you for a drink, you would have asked him and he would have given you living water."

¹¹"Sir," the woman said, "you have nothing to draw with and the well is deep. Where can you get this living water? ¹²Are you greater than our father Jacob, who gave us the well and drank from it himself, as did also his sons and his livestock?"

¹³Jesus answered, "Everyone who drinks this water will be thirsty again, ¹⁴but whoever drinks the water I give them will never thirst. Indeed, the water I give them will become in them a spring of water welling up to eternal life."

¹⁵The woman said to him, "Sir, give me this water so that I won't get thirsty and have to keep coming here to draw water."

I don't know about you but I am not a huge fan of long, drawn out conversations.

Perhaps this could be a product of being a man; ladies seem to have more of an appreciation for these kinds of things. Even still, I could attribute this to my own lack of patience – I think all of us husbands could use more of it.

While lengthy discussions do sometimes have merit, I have often found them to not be the most productive. The reasons for this vary but probably the most common is that one or more of the individuals in the exchange is simply not listening. Have you ever had this experience?

Listening, like a good cake, has layers. This concept may seem foreign; although after careful thought, it is rather intuitive. As the expression "read between the lines" suggests, listening does not only apply to someone's literal words but also their implications – the attitude and intentions behind them. Says well-known Chinese church leader, Watchman Nee, "When you listen, you need to be able to decipher three different kinds of words: the words spoken, those unspoken and those hidden within their spirit."[26]

In cultivating this kind of listening, we make these conversations more effective. Yes, there's potential for them to be shorter. The truth of the matter, though, is that plenty of conversations have gone short because of a lack of listening. Our effectiveness is not gauged by a stopwatch but our ability to address the *root* of an issue versus the *fruit*. This is what Jesus did with the Samaritan woman.

We will find out more about this woman as the conversation pro-gresses, but Jesus knew enough to go for the jugular right from the beginning. She had come to this well at midday to be undisturbed in her retrieval of water, of course running into Jesus. As he sat there, tired from his journey, he asks her for water. This, however, was a set up. Their conversation had nothing to do with Jesus being thirsty, instead having everything to do with this woman's thirst. The water he offered her was able to truly satisfy, addressing the real issue.

From her responses, it is clear that this woman was only focused on the fruit of her issue. Jesus' references to the spiritual were met with the pragmatic and natural. Her concerns migrated from the taboo nature of their

26   Nee, W. (1988). *The character of God's workman*. Richmond, VA: Christian Fellowship.

exchange, to Jesus' inability to draw from the well and, finally, her retirement from her midday sojourns to Jacob's well. These preoccupations, however, were the result of what she lacked - the living water Jesus mentions.

Husbands, let us heed this all-important lesson Jesus teaches us:

As husbands, we must navigate conversations to find the root issue.

As I mentioned at the close of the last chapter, we cannot avoid conversations that are serious or even difficult – these are the discussions that we should, in large part, initiate. Whether or not these conversations will occur is not the issue, rather it is how they are navigated. Being prone to offense or insistent upon being right will only frustrate matters. The question that should surface in the mind of every husband as our wives express challenges, complaints and fears is this: *What is the reason we are having this conversation?* If you do not ask this question quickly enough, a matter that could have been resolved in an hour can last a week.

While I am still growing in this, this was a struggle early on in marriage. When experiencing conflict, my default was to point to the fact of the matter rather than the heart of it. One such time, my wife had sent me a text message while I was away at a work event. When I received it, I reckoned I was not in a position to immediately respond, especially because the subject matter was not "urgent." Unfortunately, several hours had passed with no response, which was a topic of discussion when I arrived at home late in the evening. Of course, I made the matter about the importance of the actual message; to me, it was not urgent, and I was "too busy" to respond. Our conversation, however, should not have been at all about the content of the message, rather the importance of the messenger.

My critical error was thinking that as long as I could sufficiently address what was being said, I had done my duty. Essentially, this is how these conversations translated; they were more a chore than an opportunity for understanding and depth of intimacy. If I was listening to her heart – if

I was listening *with* my heart – I would have known to affirm her value to me and assure her of being my top priority. The root issue is always a matter of the heart, and we must diligently pursue dialogue on this plain in order discover it and deal with it properly.

Much like ourselves, our wives will frequently be unaware of the root issue. They will espouse their thoughts and feelings but not necessarily the source. It is much easier to talk about the fruit, because it is visible and tangible. Getting under the surface takes work, it takes practice. The only way to really cultivate this is using every conversation as an opportunity to listen on a heart level.

All the Samaritan woman knew was that she did not want to come to this well anymore. She was probably tired of the physical and social strain of doing so at midday alone. Even if Jesus promised her a daily delivery of water to her doorstep for the rest of her life, the issues which brought her to the well would still remain. While we can often be tempted to "fix" the issue, in essence remaining on the surface, we must resist this tendency.

Suffice it to say, the intimacy in our marriages depends on it.

CHAPTER 18:

"KNOWING HER" (V. 16-19)

16He told her, "Go, call your husband and come back."

17"I have no husband," she replied.

Jesus said to her, "You are right when you say you have no husband. 18The fact is, you have had five husbands, and the man you now have is not your husband. What you have just said is quite true."

19"Sir," the woman said, "I can see that you are a prophet."

Intimacy can often be misconstrued as something merely physical, but it is much more holistic in nature.

When you are intimate with your spouse, you are connected at the deepest level, physically, emotionally and spiritually. To be intimate is, indeed, *to know*. In fact, when the first couple came together physically, the Scriptures describe it the following way:

> *Now Adam knew Eve his wife, and she conceived and bore Cain, saying, "I have gotten a man with the help of the LORD."*
> (Genesis 4:1 ESV)

Intimacy, in every sense, is about knowing. It is a knowledge that can only be experienced when there is true vulnerability. The walls of insecurity must be torn down and, hopefully, not rebuilt like the those of Jericho (1 Kings 16:34). As husbands, what helps us to maintain these channels of intimacy is what we do with the things we know.

Jesus, in talking to the Samaritan woman, makes a very interesting conversational segue. She had already made clear her desire to not have to return to the well to draw water. That she was doing so in the first place was already a commentary on her relational status. If she had a husband, and if he was even a half decent man, it would have been him coming to the well to draw the water they needed. Knowing this, Jesus tells her to go get her husband.

His request for the woman to go and bring back her husband was strategic. If he had only asked if she was married, she would have had the opportunity to lie; one could imagine the shame which led her to the well at this time of day also motivating her to hide the truth from a total stranger. Clearly, since Jesus already knew the truth, it was not merely about him knowing. She needed to understand that Jesus knew *her*, much more than she realized. This was so the case that after he reads her mail, she correctly perceives him to be a prophet.

Jesus was not using this woman's past as a weapon. Instead, he was using his intimate knowledge of her life in order to gain greater access to her heart. He did not make the trip to Samaria to merely have a surface conversation. No, this was going to go as deep as the root issue required. Strangers, though, do not get to the root. In fact, they do not really get any-where. People who have a sense of intimate knowledge, and also demonstrate it, are allowed this access.

Our lesson from Jesus, then, is this:

As husbands, our wives should see that we know them.

Each husband is, of course, privy to things concerning his wife that no one else knows – this is the nature of marriage. There should be things that only spouses share, although I would not say entrées are one of them.

Even still, our wives do have others in their lives who "know" them. They have interests, favorites and quirks that are common knowledge amongst both friends and family. These things should not just be random facts to a husband, rather actionable intel. As we aspire to foster greater intimacy, we are to convey what we already know of our wives in ways which clearly display this knowledge.

If you are like me, buying a birthday gift can be one of the most daunting activities. Sure, it is typically rewarding in the end, knowing you were able to bless someone. The feeling of not knowing what to get and the thought of the recipient not liking the gift, however, is probably why many of us have given gift cards. While they certainly do make matters simple, a gift card is typically not something you give to your wife for her birthday.

For my wife's most recent birthday, I was at a total loss. She is a very content person, and often has a hard time even knowing what she wants – this makes ordering at a restaurant very adventurous. After searching online for inspiration, I simply decided to go to a store. Of the stores she likes, there is one fairly close to our home; I made a covert visit while running errands one day.

After entering the store, I still did not have a clue what to buy. How can you give a gift to someone who does not even know what they want?

Then I started to think about *her*; her interests, favorites and quirks. My focus had been on the gift and not the actual recipient. Once I had this change in perspective, choosing became rather easy. After I had surprised her with her gifts, she commented that they were among the best she had ever received.

Had I bought her things that were more expensive?

Yes.

Ironically, a few months prior, I had bought her a gift worth almost twice as much as the ones she received for her birthday. To date, I still have not seen her use it.

It was not about the cost, however, rather tapping into her personhood and displaying my appreciation for her uniqueness. In truth, this does not even take money; it takes thought and proactivity.

Intimacy is not just about knowing the good things, though. Truer to the conversation between Jesus and the Samaritan woman is the notion of knowing things our wives would rather keep a secret. This woman had five husbands. That's right, five. We are not told the reason each of those marriages ended but the stigma of having five husbands is one that crosses time and culture.

While she may have given up on marriage, it does not seem that she had given up on men as a whole. Jesus makes mention of the man she is with currently. It is certainly no crime to be seeing someone. He is highlighting, however, the apparent compromising nature of their relationship. The broken promises of her past no doubt led to her lowered standards in the present.

We all have things about ourselves that make us insecure. If this is the case for us husbands, we should know that it is probably doubly so for our wives. What intimacy allows is for us to show that we are aware of the things that make them insecure and persist in relationship. Jesus knew the Samaritan woman's past and present, and still purposefully pursued her – oh what love from our Savior!

Husbands, our wives want to know that we know them. Not only does Christ's example provide us with inspiration and instruction, it also highlights this great relational need.

When we show our wives that they are truly known, it postures their hearts to not only receive our love but also our influence and authority.

CHAPTER 19:

"INSTRUCTING HER" (V. 20-26)

²⁰*Our ancestors worshiped on this mountain, but you Jews claim that the place where we must worship is in Jerusalem."*

²¹ *"Woman," Jesus replied, "believe me, a time is coming when you will worship the Father neither on this mountain nor in Jerusalem. ²²You Samaritans worship what you do not know; we worship what we do know, for salvation is from the Jews. ²³Yet a time is coming and has now come when the true worshipers will worship the Father in the Spirit and in truth, for they are the kind of worshipers the Father seeks. ²⁴God is spirit, and his worshipers must worship in the Spirit and in truth."*

²⁵*The woman said, "I know that Messiah" (called Christ) "is coming. When he comes, he will explain everything to us."*

²⁶*Then Jesus declared, "I, the one speaking to you—I am he."*

At the beginning of this section, we talked about God's creative intent for men to be leaders, the culmination of this being the role of husband. As such, they are to be the protectors of their families. They are to work to provide for them. Men are to be the pastors of their homes.

In the literal sense, the word "pastor" is a shepherding term. It can be used of one who has been entrusted with the care of a flock or herd. Naturally, shepherds feed and protect their flocks, ensuring they have plenty of grass and a safe environment to graze. Spiritually speaking, the church leaders we envision upon hearing this word do the same. They are concerned about the nourishment and well-being of those entrusted to their care, and their means of attending to both is the word of God.

While the *office* of pastor is reserved for those who have been appointed by the Holy Spirit over a congregation (Acts 20:28) and whose authority is acknowledged within the church (Hebrews 13:17), the *function* of a pastor is to be present at every home address. Paul speaks to this function as he continues addressing husbands in Ephesians:

> [25]*Husbands, love your wives, just as Christ loved the church and gave himself up for her* [26]*to make her holy, cleansing her by the washing with water through the word* . . . (Ephesians 5:25-26)

Yes, Jesus gave himself for the church so it could be made holy, but he also gave her the word. To give his life and not leave behind a will would have been irresponsible, even if he did rise from the dead. Jesus was not only making the ultimate sacrifice in order to save the lives of those he loved, he also wanted to make sure they knew how to live the new lives he was purchasing for them. He says in his high priestly prayer to the Father, "Make them holy by your truth; teach them your word, which is truth" (John 17:17 NLT). We see this in action in his conversation with the Samaritan woman.

Recognizing she was in the presence of no ordinary stranger, this woman saw an opportunity. For years, Jews and Samaritans had nothing to do with each other, each purporting their own cultural traditions and theological beliefs. This woman probably had no contact with a Jewish man, yet alone a prophet. If Jesus was an authority from God, he would surely be able to bring clarity on a topic as important as worship.

To this woman, worship was a lot like real estate: it was all about the location. In her mind, and in the minds of many, worshipping God was only an activity for the mountaintop. Mount Zion in Jerusalem was magnificent, the place where Solomon had formerly built his temple, and where Herod's temple was presently. It was not, however, where Moses had pronounced blessing upon God's people before entering Canaan (Deuteronomy 11:29). To Samaritans, to this woman, it was Mount Gerizim that gave them their ties to the patriarchs, especially their father, Jacob. This is the place where they would worship.

Jesus' response to this woman's statement is among the most popular passages of Scripture. Not only does he invalidate the claims of the Samaritans, he also challenges the premise of their discussion. It was to be expected that this woman would be wrong about worship; after all, Jesus did say, "You Samaritans worship what you do not know." He, though, takes this opportunity to teach her about the true nature of worship. It is not based on physical location but on spiritual connection.

In all honesty, the conversation does seem to take a random turn. They went from talking about the woman's five ex-husbands and current boyfriend to the correct location for corporate worship. Jesus, being the Good Shepherd, could not resist cleansing her of wrong thinking with the truth of God's word. In doing so, he models for us what it is to be a personal pastor to our wives, teaching us the following:

**As husbands, we should be able to instruct our wives
in matters of worship.**

We live in a day where spirituality is more readily associated with women than with men. The image we have of churches on Sunday mornings is one where men are vastly outnumbered by their female counterparts. While this reality has changed over the years,[27] the devotional habits of Christian men and women add to this narrative. According to a 2014 study by Pew Research Center, 74% of women said they prayed daily compared to only

---

27   Burge, R. (2020, March 04). Guest column: Behind the steep decline in church attendance among women. Retrieved August 13, 2020, from https://www.barna.com/changes-behind-the-scenes/

60% of men. When it comes to reading Scripture at least once-a-week, 49% of women claimed this was the case versus 40% of men.[28]

This perception, these statistics, still do not negate the role of spiritual leadership men are to have in the home. It could be that our wives have a greater capacity for devotion; even the apostles fled from Jesus while the assortment of Marys stood at the foot of the cross (John 19:25). Even still, he sent Mary Magdelene back to the apostles to empower them with the good news. Jesus wants each husband to be empowered to not only be examples of devotion but also spiritual educators, imparting truth into the lives of our brides.

Having this responsibility on a husband's shoulders means it is possible to acheive. Perhaps you are a husband reading this and do not feel equipped to be the pastor of your home. The reasons for this vary: being new to the faith, having diffiiculty reading the Bible or even being intimidated by the spiritual maturity of your wife. Do not be dismayed; everyone has to start somewhere, and we are all on a progressive journey of Christ-likeness.

When aspiring to be a fit instructor, the best place to begin is with the disposition of a willing student. Again, even Jesus had to grow in wisdom (Luke 2:52). He was willing to sit at the feet of the teachers of his day, and we should do the same. It can be difficult, at times, for us men to listen to someone else; not wanting to appear inferior or ignorant is often what halts our progress. There are people, regardless, who are assigned to our spiritual development (pastors, small group leaders, disciplers). Not only should we embrace them but also appreciate them (Galatians 6:6).

There are even things we can learn from our wives. Listening to them should not make us feel emasculated, rather more effective. Many husbands have made the mistake of doing the opposite and regretted it – just ask Pilate (Matthew 27:19). After all, the apostle Paul seemed to think

---

28   Religion in America: U.S. religious Data, demographics and statistics. (2020, September 09). Retrieved August 13, 2020, from https://www.pewforum.org/religious-landscape-study/christians/christian/gender-composition/#beliefs-and-practices

there would be instances where we would learn from each other. He writes to the Colossians:

> *Let the message of Christ dwell among you richly as you teach*
> *and admonish one another with all wisdom through psalms,*
> *hymns, and songs from the Spirit, singing to God with gratitude*
> *in your hearts.* (Colossians 3:16)

Interestingly enough, he distinctly addresses husbands and wives shortly thereafter (v. 18-19).

Ultimately, the place we should go to become the pastors of our homes is God himself. Jesus spent time in prayer and the Scriptures, qualifying him to provide guidance to the most lost of sheep. When talking to the Samaritan woman, he did not critique her choice of worship location. His feedback was that she, and the other Samaritans, did not truly know the God they claimed to worship. Knowing him – personally, deeply, intimately – is foundational for any role of spiritual leadership, and the home is no exception.

So, what next?

Do what I did when I needed to "restart" my relationship with God.

Having left Detroit to start my freshman year of college, I arrived with not the greatest of intentions. In my mind, I was free to do whatever I wanted. There was no parent, there was no God, who was going to stop me. My flirtation with sin was, however, rather short-lived; thank God for his mercy.

In getting my spiritual life back on track, I knew I needed to become serious about one thing: reading my Bible. Of course, I did not have one. One of my last rites in Detroit was ceremonially leaving my only Bible on my nightstand. Shakespeare would have had an appreciation for the monologue which resulted in me leaving it, as I said to myself, "To take or not to take."

Buying a Bible was arguably one of the greatest favors I have ever done myself. It, quite literally, was an investment I was making in my spiritual life, one which has paid dividends ever since. Not only do I still use this Bible (though the spine is being held together by scotch tape) but also this decision situated me on a trajectory leading to the very words you are reading. When we commit ourselves to God's instructions for worship, it becomes the result of our lives, and others are instructed by the lives we live for him.

The Samaritan woman expected the Messiah to explain everything to her; Jesus was, of course, able to do so. While we husbands might not have all the answers, we do have a connection to the one who does. He will lead us as we aspire to lead our homes, providing our wives with a powerful model of worship.

CHAPTER 20:

"UNASHAMED" (V. 27)

Just then his disciples returned and were surprised to find him talking with a woman. But no one asked, "What do you want?" or "Why are you talking with her?"

Just as things started to get good, here come the disciples.

This interruption would prove to be the official end of the conversation between Jesus and the Samaritan woman. From experience, we all know how difficult it is to maintain conversational flow post stoppage. It does seem, though, Jesus revealing himself to her as the Messiah was a fitting conclusion.

The Twelve, upon their departure to the nearest town, had left Jesus alone. Since it was an unusual time of day for anyone to come to a well to draw water, they did not expect him to have company. Their surprise was doubled when discovering he was talking alone with a woman.

In rabbinical tradition, it was taboo for any teacher to talk with a woman in public. This is based on one of the precepts that says, "Let no one talk with a woman in the street, no not with his own wife."[29] Women, generally speaking, were not held in high regard in those days but there was a particular bias when it came to religious education. No rabbi would ever

---

29   Cambridge Bible for Schools and Colleges on John 4:27

be seen in public talking to a woman. Not only was it against the rules, it was also considered a waste of time.

That John notes how the disciples did not ask "What do you want?" or "Why are you talking with her?" is only an indicator of their actual thoughts. It was bad enough they were breaking one social rule in going through Samaria; they certainly did not expect Jesus to break another in talking to this woman. If the term awkward silence ever applied to a situation, it is this one.

Jesus, while he need not issue a reply, does speak volumes. If he knew enough to ensure he would intersect with this woman, at this well, at this time, on this particular day, he also knew the disciples would return to find him speaking to her. This did not seem to be a concern in the least. While the privacy he and this woman had afforded them an opportunity to have a substantive conversation, he was not trying to keep her a secret – we have this story recorded in the Scriptures for this exact reason. No rabbinical rule or social stigma would detract from his deliberate decision to be publicly seen with her.

As husbands, and those living in the 21 century, we are not necessarily battling the hurdles Jesus had to climb. No one would shame us for talking to our own wives in public. Even interracial marriages are less contentious now than in the past. Jesus, still, does teach us something by unashamedly being seen with this woman:

As husbands, we should take pride in our bride.

Each of our wives is God's unique gift to us. The day she walked down the aisle was, perhaps, the pinnacle of this realization. All the guests in attendance literally stood as she made her grand entrance. With the biggest of smiles (in my case, a bucket of tears), we watched as our family and friends acknowledged just how special was the woman to whom we would pledge our covenant love. No one, however, thought she was as special as we did.

As years pass, children are born, and through ups and downs, we are to hold on to this view. Truly, a gift does not cease being a gift due to the passage of time. For every man who has bought an engagement ring, I know you hope this is the case. To this day, it brings me great joy to see Heidi wearing her ring. Having our wives in our lives should bring us joy on a daily basis.

Famously, Proverbs 31 speaks to this subject. While most of the Proverbs are written by Solomon, this chapter was penned by King Lemuel, as inspired by his mother (31:1). He dedicates verses 10-31 to speak of the kind of woman fit for a king. She is wise, a hard worker and cares for her household. The discourse ends with the celebration of this woman:

[28]*Her children arise and call her blessed;*

her husband also, and he praises her:

[29]*"Many women do noble things,*

but you surpass them all."

[30]*Charm is deceptive, and beauty is fleeting;*

but a woman who fears the Lord is to be praised.

[31]*Honor her for all that her hands have done, and let her works*
bring her praise at the city gate. (Proverbs 31:28-31)

My brothers, if our wives are worthy to be chosen, they are worthy to be praised. This first happens in private, in moments of solitude and intimacy. Here, we have an opportunity to feed her soul by esteeming her. Without an audience, it shows that our celebration is authentic.

How can we praise her to others but never say to her a flattering word? Will this even happen in public if it is not cultivated in private?

Admittedly, this has not always been an area of strength for me. If we are not careful, selfishness and ungodly competition can get in the way of our vocation to praise our wives. That's right; praising our wives is a part of our "vocation" as husbands. We all need to be affirmed but especially our wives. They need to know they are valued, cared for and desired. Knowing this, we should be their greatest source of encouragement.

Praise of our wives should also be contagious in the home. That "her children arise and call her blessed," I'm sure, has everything to do with the disposition of her husband. We should not only praise our wives in private but also make it a point to do so in front of our children. This dispels division and communicates a unified front – we have all seen how kids try to pit parents against one another. Also, this *elevates* the influence of our wives in the home. Yes, she already has influence just by virtue of being mom. If the man in charge esteems her, though, there is nowhere for her to go but up.

Lastly, and true to Jesus' exchange with the Samaritan woman, our praise happens in public. According to Lemuel, it is, indeed, "her works" which bring her praise at the city gate. My wife is amazing because she is amazing, not because I say so. Still, it does make sense for me to be the one to express this.

Interestingly enough, there is something about the city gate we should not overlook:

Her husband is respected at the city gate, where he takes his seat among the elders of the land. (Proverbs 31:23)

The Proverbs 31 woman is praised at the city gate because of the seat her husband occupies. He cannot help but be boastful about his bride, and the most important people in the land know about her.

The celebration of our wives should permeate the most public of places. Our coworkers, friends and associates should all know of her wonderful works. This, of course, also means they will accompany us in public. As we take our wives on dates, they should feel as if they are the most important person in the world. Even when running errands together, people should know that we are proud to be with the one we love. Truly, every husband should be able to say to their wife, "Many women do noble things, but you surpass them all."

Jesus was not ashamed to be found publicly with the Samaritan woman. He in fact planned on it. This was an act of esteem unheard of in his day. She was important enough to take a detour, be in the hot sun and break some stringent social cues. From her response, it was pretty apparent just how valued Jesus made her feel.

May this be so of all of us.

CHAPTER 21:

"LEADING WELL" (V. 28-30)

28Then, leaving her water jar, the woman went back to the town and said to the people, 29"Come, see a man who told me everything I ever did. Could this be the Messiah?" 30They came out of the town and made their way toward him.

This woman experienced a lot of disappointment in her life.

I do not know what it feels like to have been married five times – I hope I never do. It does seem that I would feel a sense of shame or even hopelessness. We can presume both of the Samaritan woman based on her choices. Not only did she determine to come to the well at a time guaranteeing her social isolation, but she also decided to be romantically involved with someone that was not her husband; perhaps he was even someone else's.

It is a shame we do not know more about her past. Indeed, we are not given the reason each of her marriages ended (or her name for that matter). We can, nonetheless, deduce a few things from the Scriptures.

Contrary to her current relational choice, it does not seem indiscretion, on her part, was the reason any of those marriages ended. If the treatment of the woman in John 8 is any indicator, there would have been no hesitation to stone her if this was the case. While the Jewish leaders who instigated this scene seem merciless, they were actually on firm legal footing (despite their differences, Jews and Samaritans both honored the books of Moses):

If a man commits adultery with another man's wife – with the wife of his neighbor – both the adulterer and the adulteress are to be put to death. (Leviticus 20:10)

Divorcing due to adultery would not just have ended the Samaritan woman's marriages, it very likely would have ended her life. So, what could be the reason for the end of each of her five marriages?

It is possible that each of her husbands died. The Sadducees, in trying to disprove the resurrection to Jesus (I'm sure you can see the humor in this), created a scenario where a woman marries seven brothers who each pass away; this is because of a law that required a man's brother to marry his wife after dying with no son (Deuteronomy 25:5). There are even instances of this in Israel's history. Tamar, Judah's daughter-in-law, married two of his sons for this reason (Genesis 38:6-10).

Yes, death remains a possibility for the demise of these marriages, at least in part. What is interesting about the exchange between Jesus and this woman, though, is a couple of key omissions: there is no mention of children and no evidence any of these husbands were related. There being no sign of children would lend itself to the scenario created by the Sadducees; this woman would have then gone to the next brother. We, of course, do not know if these husbands were related or not but it seems this detail would have been mentioned. If she does have children, coming to the well in the middle of the day without them does not seem to be the best idea.

Maybe death is not why they parted after all?

There remains another possible cause for the end of her marriages. Divorce was a hot button topic in Jesus' day. He discussed marriage and divorce on multiple occasions with the teachers of the law. In one instance, he is asked by the Pharisees, "Is it lawful for a man to divorce his wife for any and every reason" (Matthew 19:3)?

This question is representative of two schools of thought. The school of Shammai argued that divorce was only permitted in the case of adultery. Conversely, the school of Hillel believed in a husband's right to divorce his wife for even the most trivial of reasons.[30] While Jesus, essentially, agrees with the school of Shammai (Matthew 19:8-9), there were many who held the opposite view. When reading the writings of Moses, this was, perhaps, for good reason:

> [1]*If a man marries a woman who becomes displeasing to him because he finds something indecent about her, and he writes her a certificate of divorce, gives it to her and sends her from his house, [2]and if after she leaves his house she becomes the wife of another man, [3]and her second husband dislikes her and writes her a certificate of divorce, gives it to her and sends her from his house, or if he dies, [4]then her first husband, who divorced her, is not allowed to marry her again after she has been defiled. That would be detestable in the eyes of the Lord. Do not bring sin upon the land the Lord your God is giving you as an inheritance.* (Deuteronomy 24:1-4)

Adultery and death could have been the reasons for the Samaritan woman's five husbands. Yet, it seems most likely these men were inspired by this passage, sending her away because they simply found her "displeasing." The reasons for this are infinite. Maybe she was not a good cook? Or maybe she was not very clean? Could she have snored?

We might not know the exact cause but each possible answer draws the same conclusion: this woman was unwanted. She may have been deemed good enough to marry, and this on five occasions, but not to keep. Interestingly, based on the law, there were no grounds for any of her ex-husbands to change their minds. If he wrote her a certificate of divorce, he was also consenting to not remarrying her after she had been another man's wife. Even if she wanted to go back, she could not.

---

30   Barnes' Notes on the Bible on Matthew 19:3

Five husbands and a likely fling later, she meets Jesus. It goes without saying that he is different from any man she has ever met. He demonstrated a pursuit that brought him to Jacob's well at the hottest time of day. His willingness to go to the conversational depths was fully on display.

Jesus, truly, knew her. This was so the case that she commented, "Come, see a man who told me everything I ever did." He was not only willing to be seen talking to this woman in public but also took the time to teach her, which no rabbi would have ever done. Her experience with Jesus was quite the opposite from the five husbands who left her.

As this woman's conversation with Jesus ends, she does the unthinkable. After coming to Jacob's well in total isolation to draw water, she tosses her water jar and goes back into town to make a public announcement! Her shame and despair may have prompted reclusive living but her encounter with Jesus broke those chains. There was such a display of freedom in her message about the Messiah, the townspeople actually left town to go see him. This woman became the first documented evangelist to Samaria, and it was because of how Jesus viewed her, talked to her and treated her.

Men of God, my prayer is for us to emulate Jesus' powerful example. This woman's life was in utter shambles prior to his arrival. He, however, saw a purpose that was beyond her pain, and unlocking it led to the proclamation of Jesus as Messiah to the Samaritans. Let us, then, take note of this:

As husbands, our leadership should leave our wives free to be who God has called them to be. This will, in turn, esteem us in their eyes and the eyes of others.

A lot of times when we get married, we think of the immense blessing we have just received in our wives. Naturally, we are excited to experience a new standard of living, having an expectancy for our brides to enrich us in many ways. Home cooked meals, emotional and financial support, and unbridled displays of affection become a new norm for us former bachelors.

We cannot ignore, however, the immense responsibility we have to our wives. Our role is to lead them, and leading always implies a direction and a destination. As our wives follow us, they should be journeying towards their unique calling in Christ. God bringing us together means they are to reach this spiritual goal as a byproduct of our union. Indeed, as husbands, we are entrusted with the stewardship of our wives' calling.

This certainly does not mean that we do not have a calling of our own. It does mean, however, their calling should be our priority. While Jesus had his own assignment from God the Father, Paul makes it clear that his sacrifice and revelation of God's word had a spiritual aim for his bride:

> . . . to present her to himself as a radiant church, without
> stain or wrinkle or any other blemish, but holy and blameless.
> (Ephesians 5:27)

Though every Christ follower can expect to spend eternity with God and each other, we will, first, make an individual appearance before the judgment seat of Christ to give an account for our lives. When each of our wives makes her appearance, our influence and leadership will have much to do with her report.

What a sobering thought.

While this call is weighty, it is also a wonderful opportunity! If you feel at all about your wife what I do mine, I know you believe there is immense potential for her to be used by God; he is, in fact, now using her in more ways than we probably know. Much like the Samaritan woman, though, sometimes there are hurdles. Past hurts, insecurities and wrong thinking can hinder anyone from pursing their God-given purpose, and definitely our wives. Before operating in their unique spiritual vein, our wives need to feel comfortable in their own skin. As we love, appreciate and lead them, this becomes increasingly the case.

One person that really demonstrates this is a brother by the name of Dave. You may have heard of his wife, Joyce…Meyer.

Joyce had a rough early life. Her father abused her sexually as a young girl and she had already been divorced by the age of 23; her husband was, tragically, unfaithful. She met Dave Meyer soon after her first marriage ended, and they married rather quickly. After finding her footing in Christian ministry as a teacher, Joyce's influence began to expand, going from teaching early morning Bible classes to having a 15-mintue radio program on six stations regionally.

Having endured the struggles of starting the non-profit, "Life in the Word," Dave saw an opportunity for Joyce's teaching ministry to go beyond radio and conferences. He disclosed in a 1999 interview that in 1993 God "opened his heart to [him]," adding, "I could feel the hurts of the world." From there, he decided Joyce's message should go international on television. Starting initially on WGN in Chicago and Black Entertainment Television (BET), the program *Enjoying Everyday Life* now reaches people all around the world.[31]

Our influence as husbands cannot be understated. While every woman does not have a story as littered with heartache as Joyce Meyer or the Samaritan woman, many actually do. For those that do not, there is often some difficulty posing a challenge to their progress in God. We are assigned to be agents of healing and hope; healing is needed for the traumas of life and hope to cultivate expectation for the future in Christ. Only the Lord knows what is truly possible when both of these things work powerfully in tandem.

Just think of how Dave Meyer was used in Joyce's life. Better yet, think of how Jesus was used in the Samaritan woman's life.

When we serve our wives in this way, inevitably, they demonstrate their appreciation. It is, surely, not our aim to gain applause. We do what we do because we love our wives, and desire to fill the shoes left by our Savior.

---

31   Smith, B., & Tuft, C. (2003, November 15). Meyer traces her fervor to early abuse, alcohol. Retrieved August 21, 2020, from https://web.archive.org/web/20060127003333/http://www.stltoday.com/stltoday/news/special/joycemeyer.nsf/0/1D29266A7F855B2886256DDF00701F8A?OpenDocument

Still, a husband who leads like Jesus will seldom experience ingratitude. Not only will we have our wives' respect but also a glowing reputation.

This was certainly the case with Jesus.

> [39]*Many of the Samaritans from that town believed in him because of the woman's testimony, "He told me everything I ever did." [40]So when the Samaritans came to him, they urged him to stay with them, and he stayed two days. [41]And because of his words many more became believers.*
>
> [42]*They said to the woman, "We no longer believe just because of what you said; now we have heard for ourselves, and we know that this man really is the Savior of the world."* (John 4:39-42)

The Samaritan woman could not help but tell her fellow Samaritans about Jesus. It was not that it was at all convenient for her. Again, she left her water jar, made a trip into town and risked the ridicule of being a woman, much less one with a reputation, making a public address. Nevertheless, she took a group back to Jacob's well to see the one she held in such high regard. They, too, saw in Jesus what this woman saw: The Messiah.

While none of us will ever garner this level of acclaim, this principle still stands. Just recently, while reading the news in the morning, I came across an article that could not have been more apropos. In it, *Duck Dynasty* star, Sadie Robertson, talks of two gentlemen who laughed when she was sharing a story of a time when "a guy really hurt" her. She explained that she had not revealed this level of detail at any previous speaking engagement, this being a particularly emotional telling.

After offering an initial retort, Roberson realized that her husband, Christian Huff, had also come to her defense. She comments,

> *"I quickly realized I wasn't the only one who stood up for myself," Robertson recalled. "This husband of mine took them*

outside, and no, did not hit them, but called them to be better
men. He called them to maturity and to greatness."

The title of this article, perhaps, speaks most loudly and appropriately on the subject: *Sadie Robertson Praises Husband for Confronting 2 Men Who Laughed While She Was Sharing a Story.*[32]

Being a husband is no joke, but we are able to do so in a way that is celebrated by our wives and, most importantly, by our Lord.

Not only has Jesus given us husbands an amazing example but also an amazing empowerment. Think about it: we could not truly be told to "love our wives, just as Christ loved the church" if it were not possible! He is cheering each of us on as we endeavor to emulate him in this area of our lives. What we need to succeed is to be good at playing, "Follow the Leader." As long as we do not break the chain, we'll be in good shape:

> *But I want you to understand that the head of every man is*
> *Christ, the head of a wife is her husband, and the head of Christ*
> *is God.* (1 Corinthians 11:3 ESV)

---

32   Stone, N. (2020, August 18). Sadie Robertson praises her husband for Confronting 2 men who laughed while she was sharing a personal story. Retrieved August 21, 2020, from https://people.com/tv/sadie-robertson-praises-husband-for-confronting-2-men-who-laughed-while-she-was-sharing-a-story/

SECTION FIVE:

"AN AMAZING FATHER" – JESUS THE FATHER

Isaiah 53:10

> *Yet it was the Lord's will to crush him and cause him to suffer,*
>
> *and though the Lord makes his life an offering for sin,*
>
> *he will see his offspring and prolong his days,*
>
> *and the will of the Lord will prosper in his hand.*

Just as in a relay race, in life, there is an eventual passing of the baton.

As individuals, even if we run with all our might, we are only as strong as the next runner. Preparing our children for their leg of the race, then, is crucial not only to their success but our legacy.

Jesus was not a father by natural means, but Isaiah reveals he does have offspring spiritually speaking. When talking with his disciples, Jesus makes it clear that he has come to reveal the Father (John 14:7-11) – in fact, he and the Father are one (John 10:30). As such, he walked with the Father's heart, demeanor and disposition. In both seeing and knowing Jesus, indeed, we see and know the Father as well.

Jesus shows us our race is not truly complete if our children are not prepared to run. In his interactions with his "children" throughout the gospels, we see him praising, protecting and pursuing them. We will, then, examine some unique instances to learn from Jesus' fatherly heart.

CHAPTER 22:

"THE GREATEST"

Our son, Marshall, being born was one of the greatest experiences I have ever had in life.

At the time of this writing, he is our only child. Though a blur, I still have a pretty clear picture of his early life because of this. The first time I held him almost did not feel real – I have probably picked him up hundreds of times since then. Each time, he seems to be a little heavier, more verbal and more expressive than the last. Children sure do seem to grow up fast.

Currently, Heidi and I are in a season where discipline is becoming more of a reality. Marshall may have once been a docile little infant who just laid on a blanket, but now he is a rambunctious toddler who pretends he does not know the meaning of the word, "no." Despite all of the food throwing, hitting and screaming, he remains the apple of our eyes. He is the delight of our home, and we could not be prouder to be his parents.

The way my wife and I both feel about Marshall is how Jesus feels about every child, especially those who are his own. In a conversation with the disciples, he shares his heart concerning children:

> [1]*At that time the disciples came to Jesus and asked, "Who, then, is the greatest in the kingdom of heaven?"* [2]*He called a little child to him, and placed the child among them.* [3]*And he said: "Truly I tell you, unless you change and become like*

little children, you will never enter the kingdom of heaven.
⁴Therefore, whoever takes the lowly position of this child is
the greatest in the kingdom of heaven. ⁵And whoever welcomes
one such child in my name welcomes me. (Matthew 18:1-5)

Perhaps, in the proceeding exchange, Jesus conveys an esteem that is higher than any other.

The disciples, unfortunately preoccupied by position and status, ask a pretty audacious question. They had been with Jesus for some time now but he still had much to teach them. In one way, their question does not even make sense. Clearly, in a kingdom, the greatest is always the king. In the kingdom of heaven, then, one would have to conclude that the greatest is Jesus.

Jesus begins to answer the question being posed by their hearts, not their lips. Truly, they were asking, "Which of *us* is the greatest in the kingdom of heaven?" Knowing this, he answers in a way that was surprising and probably offensive. He, simply, calls over a child and places him in their midst. This was definitely not the answer they were looking for, and Jesus knew they needed an explanation.

In presenting a child as the answer to the disciples' question, Jesus was debunking their conceptions of what it meant to be great. For Jewish males, their notion of greatness was a picture of a conquering king from the line of David, one who would come and eradicate the enemies of Israel. Under Roman rule in the first century, one was also inundated by the images of the soldiers who represented the world's reigning empire. These images were so prominent that the apostle Paul was likely inspired by a soldier's attire as he famously writes of the full armor of God (Ephesians 6:11-17).

Jesus could have presented a number of things in order illustrate greatness in the kingdom. He could have grabbed a sword, shield or even the Scriptures; the teachers of the law, undoubtedly, thought they were the greatest in the kingdom. While they were probably waiting to hear one of their names, Jesus did not respond with, "Peter," "James" or "John." Of all the ways Jesus could have responded, he does so with a child.

How humbling this must have been for them.

This was exactly the point! Jesus was saying that it is not bravado or even bravery that makes one great in the kingdom. It is *humility* which grants a person this honor. In fact, one will not even be admitted into the kingdom without it. This humility is best illustrated by the example of children.

Jesus had hand selected each of these men to be leaders in his kingdom movement. When it came time to bestow the kingdom's highest honor, however, he chose a child. For him, there was no better choice.

From this conversation, we glean the following fatherly principle:

As fathers, we are to esteem our children.

Most parents, if you pressed them, would confess to believing their children are the best in the world – there are parents who need not be pressed to make this known.

This, at times, can have negative consequences. We have all seen or experienced children who were spoiled, entitled or who misbehave due to the pedestal they are put on by their parents. Far too many times, these children grow into adults who possess these same qualities. Elevation without moderation is not a prescribed means of celebration.

The affirmation of a parent, nonetheless, is a powerful tool in the life of a child. Words of encouragement are often what shape the direction of our children's lives. Famously, Michael Jordan, known as perhaps the greatest basketball player of all-time, received this encouragement from his parents. They did not set out to raise a superstar but instead aspired to instill in their children the desire to "be their best and do their best." Says Delores Jordan, mother of Michael, "I always wanted my children to feel that there's nobody out there better than they are, that there's nothing you can't achieve if you work hard for it."[33]

I would say this worked out for them.

As parents, we are called to build up our children, and they should find no greater source of encouragement than ourselves. Still, there is nothing like when this comes from dad.

Anecdotally, I have seen the truth of this in the life of my little one.

Marshall is one of the happiest kids I have ever seen; he also happens to be one of the most active. Often he is running around the house, seemingly at 60 miles an hour, going from one activity to another. While we both make strides to keep step with him, Heidi, the amazing mom she is, has a gear I simply do not. In a second, she can go from reading books, to throwing balls, to building a tower. It's quite impressive.

What we often observe, though, is that when Marshall does something he deems commendable, he will *always* look in my direction. No matter what I am doing or how far away I am from him, this is always the case; my wife actually first pointed this out. This pattern has been amazing to watch ever since.

As fathers, we wield great influence when it comes to our children. I am sure similar experiences you have had to what I detailed about Marshall attest to this. Sometimes, however, the value of something is actually best assessed when it is removed.

Ronald Rohner, a Professor Emeritus of Human Development and Family Sciences and Anthropology at the University of Connecticut, has been studying parent-child relationships for over 50 years. As the Director of the Center for the Study of Interpersonal Acceptance-Rejection, and Executive Director of the International Society for Interpersonal Acceptance-Rejection, he is best known for his work on the subject beginning in 1960.

---

33   Norment, L. (1997, May). Michael's Mom: 'We Didn't Set out to Raise a super-star.'(Deloris Jordan, Mother of Basketball Star Michael Jordan)(Interview)(Cover Story). *Ebony*, *52*(7).

When commencing his research, he thought, "Like most Americans, I started out 50 years ago thinking, 'OK, sure, fathers are there and they're important in some ways, but the really important one is Mom.'"[34]

After years of study, however, Rohner's findings were, to say the least, not consistent with his original hypothesis. In an article purporting rejection by parents as the experience having the strongest and most consistent effect on personality and personality development, we also learn the following:

> *When it comes to the impact of a father's love versus that of a mother, results from more than 500 studies suggest that while children and adults often experience more or less the same level of acceptance or rejection from each parent, the influence of one parent's rejection – oftentimes the father's – can be much greater than the other's.*[35]

Perhaps you are a dad who has underestimated, devalued or been discouraged about your unique role in the home. Let me assure you, just being present is a victory in itself, based on an estimated 24.7 million children in America (33%) living absent their biological father.[36] It is, still, not enough just to be seen; we must also be heard. Our children should be very clear on how we feel about them, and we make this known through our esteem.

It is very possible that you may not be used to receiving this affirmation yourself. Fatherlessness, physically or even relationally, has probably impacted your own life. Not having a father around to esteem you, or not

34   Adams, R. (2017, December 07). 8 science-backed reasons Why dads deserve more credit. Retrieved August 30, 2020, from https://www.huffpost.com/entry/father-child-relationship_n_5558408

35   A father's love is one of the greatest influences on personality development. (2012, June 12). Retrieved August 30, 2020, from http://www.sciencedaily.com/releases/2012/06/120612101338.htm

36   U.S. Census Bureau, Current Population Survey, "Living Arrangements of Children under 18 Years/1 and Marital Status of Parents by Age, Sex, Race, and Hispanic Origin/2 and Selected Characteristics of the Child for all Children 2010." Table C3. Internet Release Date November, 2010.

hearing esteem from the father who was around, is a significant factor in our own fathering.

How can we overcome this?

In a previous chapter, we talked about Jesus' affirmation experience with the Father. When he was baptized in the Jordan River, he heard words that would very much govern the way he lived his life: "This is my Son, whom I love; with him I am well pleased" (Matthew 3:17). Joseph seemed to be a decent dad to Jesus but had Jesus not received affirmation from his earthly dad, he certainly did from his heavenly one. Yes, this experience was historically unique but the Father feels similarly about each of us:

> *In love [5]he predestined us for adoption to sonship through Jesus Christ, in accordance with his pleasure and will* (Ephesians 1:4b-5)

Knowing and experiencing this love and pleasure from the Father is foundational to affirming our own children. From there, we simply convey the Father's love and pleasure. What we receive from the Father, our kids receive from us.

Indeed, this is how Jesus lived. His constant concern was representing the Father (John 5:19), especially to those who were his own. The Father is not quiet about his love, acceptance and esteem; he parts the heavens to make this known. Jesus did so with an unnamed child in the midst of the men who would help change the world.

My fellow fathers, let us ensure we leave no stone unturned in letting our children know just how amazing they are to us.

CHAPTER 23:

"NOT MY LITTLE ONES"

Naturally, it follows that the things you value you also protect.

I am not the trendiest person when it comes to technology but I would say that I am fairly current. My Achilles heel, it seems, is always my phone. Seemingly, there is a new model that comes out every year, creating a buzz and peer pressure to purchase it or something similar.

Typically, I do not seek a new phone until my current one is pretty much unusable. One time, literally, I went into the store for a replacement and my current one could not even be turned on! On that day, and on subsequent occasions, I did something that is routine for anyone in my shoes: I, also, purchased a case. In light of the value the phone, I wanted to ensure that nothing would happen to it, in the likely event it was dropped.

What is true for many of us with our phones is also true of our homes, cars and other valuables. While there may not be cases for these things, there are security systems, safes and, of course, insurance. We know that these things are valuable enough to ensure their protection. As fathers, we know there is nothing more valuable than our children.

Jesus, assuredly, shares these sentiments.

"If anyone causes one of these little ones—those who believe in me—to stumble, it would be better for them to have a large

millstone hung around their neck and to be drowned in the
depths of the sea." (Matthew 18:6)

Following Jesus' own appraisal of the value of his children, he offers some pretty sobering words. Indeed, these words represent a deterrent to anyone who would seek the spiritual harm of those who belong to him. For the occasions where this actually transpires, he espouses how serious he is about the penalty.

What interests me about Jesus' warning is its apparent open-endedness. Warnings, typically, involve specific consequences. For instance, when you see a traffic sign indicating a certain speed limit is being photo enforced, you know the consequence of violation is a ticket in the mail. In this case, Jesus does employ a familiar illustration, as millstones were used for grinding grain and were known to be quite heavy; someone thrown into the Sea of Galilee with one of those tied around their neck would definitely drown. He, though, does not say this will happen to the individual but implies something even worse.

If it is "better" for someone to be drowned than to make one of Jesus' kids stumble, what is he willing to do when this is the case? Those who are wise will ensure they do whatever they can to not find out.

This is a side of Jesus not often discussed but is very much present throughout his life. The images portrayed of him typically involve his compassion and kindness. While he is gentle Lamb of God (John 1:29), he is also the Lion of the tribe of Judah (Revelation 5:5). As is the case with lions, Jesus needed to roar at times, especially in defense of those who belong to him. It seems, in the case of those who do his children harm, he is also willing to go on the hunt.

Quite clearly, we glean the following from Jesus:

As fathers, we our called to protect our children.

The good news for us is that we all were built with protective instincts. Not only do we intuitively protect ourselves but also those we love, especially our children. Yes, this protection is physical in nature. Keeping our children from physical harm, moreover, creating an environment of safety, is one of the most important things we can do. Those who do not often have their children removed from the home.

This protection, at the same time, is one that is holistic in nature. In addition to doing so in the physical sense, we protect our children mentally, emotionally and spiritually. Invariably, the spiritual aspect will be the driver for the others but they each have a unique facet that deserves special attention.

Protecting the mental well-being of our children entails keeping them from destructive ways of thinking. Our thoughts govern our actions and worldview, and we all have had patterns of thinking that are simply not healthy. These often stem from lies we have embraced, as told by others or formulated from experiences in our lives. Thoughts such as, "I cannot trust anyone other than myself" or "I will never amount to anything" can send one down a path of loneliness and despair. This is a path we must strenuously help our children to avoid.

Naturally, we combat lies with the truth. For fathers, there is no greater weapon to deploy as we fight for our kids. Regarding this fight, the apostle Paul offers the following:

> [4]*The weapons we fight with are not the weapons of the world. On the contrary, they have divine power to demolish strongholds.* [5]*We demolish arguments and every pretension that sets itself up against the knowledge of God, and we take captive every thought to make it obedient to Christ.* (2 Corinthians 10:4-5)

Knowing the truth, or being equipped spiritually, is how strongholds of destructive thinking are demolished. That it is a fight implies persistence on our part although Paul does tell us victory is possible. When our children's thoughts are obedient to Christ, when his truth governs their actions and worldview, we have won.

It should also be noted how the company one keeps is typically a prime factor in how one thinks. Yes, it is good for us dads to reinforce the truth to our kids. Yet, if their friends are spouting something completely opposite, our efforts could be undermined. Proverbs tells us, "Walk with the wise and become wise, for a companion of fools suffers harm" (13:20). We cannot dictate who our children choose to befriend but we can warn of danger when we see it and take action when needed.

The willingness to warn and take action not only makes us like Jesus but also can shape how our children think on a daily basis.

Our mental state is, naturally, followed by our emotions. While the two do appear inseparable, the distinction is this: our thoughts have to do with our logic and our emotions have to do with our maturity. When we comment on an individual's maturity, this often refers to someone's poise and overall demeanor. As our inner man develops, this is evidenced externally by our emotional reactions to life's occurrences.

At times, we can note that an adult has what we would consider an inappropriate emotional response to something. Perhaps, you have seen someone throw a temper tantrum fit for a toddler. While this could have been just the product of a bad day, it is likely that a piece of that individual was not nurtured and remains underdeveloped. Dealing with these tantrums at two is what can help avoid them at 30. Rest assured, the consequences are very different.

Protection in this regard, then, has to do with ensuring our children ingest things that are developmentally appropriate. We understand this concept because of the ratings on the TV shows and movies of our day. You would not allow a 10-year old to watch an R-rated movie, as there are things they should not see or hear. Honestly, I would not even watch a rated R film for those same reasons. These things can create emotional dispositions within us that are inconsistent with our stage of development, or that we simply should not have in the first place.

While emotions should never be suppressed, they can and should be tempered. Again, while it is to be expected for a two-year-old to throw a temper tantrum, you would not simply allow them to do so. As my wife often does with Marshall, we should encourage them to "use your words." Dads, at times, have to use other means of encouragement – we call this discipline. In the words of Solomon, "Folly is bound up in the heart of a child, but the rod of discipline will drive it far away" (Proverbs 22:15).

Discipline is, often, seen as merely punitive but it is much more. It is a father's means of training, reinforcing and protecting. Regarding the tantrum example, this is what, hopefully, gives our kids a healthy disposition towards anger, in that it is a valid emotion needing a measured expression. Anger unchecked, as we have too often seen, can be dangerous for a man or woman later in life. Not only can opportunities be forfeited but lives can be ruined or even ended prematurely.

As fathers, we are the protectors of our children's emotions. Not only do we keep things that are inappropriate from getting in but also teach them how to correctly process things before they come out.

What makes the protective aspect of fatherhood truly potent is the spiritual component. Yes, there are dads in the world who do not follow Jesus and still care for the physical well-being of their children. However, these children remain otherwise vulnerable without their dad's ability to protect them spiritually. These dads may be sincere but one needs more than sincerity to ensure a child's safety. What we need is awareness of the true threat facing our children, as Paul writes, "in order that Satan might not outwit us. For we are not unaware of his schemes" (2 Corinthians 2:11).

There is one who is more dangerous than the drugs, guns and gangs of the world: the devil. He is not only the enemy of our souls but he "prowls around like a roaring lion looking for someone to devour" (1 Peter 5:8) and thrives on preying on the young. His tactics include deception, accusation and temptation. If he were to have his way in the lives of our sons and daughters, it would mean their utter demise.

Yes, this is a sobering reality but there is no need to fear! While the Scripture does describe our adversary, we are also given assurance of victory, and this when we fight. In order to win, we need to know the true nature of the battle. Perhaps this is why we find the apostle Paul in the same chapter of Ephesians saying the following:

> *⁴Fathers, do not exasperate your children; instead, bring them up in the training and instruction of the Lord.* (Ephesians 6:4)
>
> *¹²For our struggle is not against flesh and blood, but against the rulers, against the authorities, against the powers of this dark world and against the spiritual forces of evil in the heavenly realms. ¹³Therefore put on the full armor of God, so that when the day of evil comes, you may be able to stand your ground, and after you have done everything, to stand.* (Ephesians 6:12-13)

The solution to protecting our children will not be found in the natural struggle but the spiritual. When we teach them the instruction of the Lord, it is as if we are picking up a spiritual sword (Ephesians 6:17), by which we assail the spiritual forces at work against them. Giving our kids the holy parameters of the Scriptures keeps them from being led astray, providing a framework from which they will not easily depart. As Proverbs famously says, "Train up a child in the way he should go; even when he is old he will not depart from it" (Proverbs 22:6 ESV).

Jesus, then, spent much of his time teaching. He wanted to ensure that those he loved had a firm grasp on the truth, especially with the father of lies inciting his children to spread his native language (John 8:44). We also see Jesus praying for his children. In John's gospel, we are given insight into the specifics of his intercession when he says, "My prayer is not that you take them out of the world but that you protect them from the evil one" (John 17:15). This is, of course, consistent with Paul's parting exhortation to the Ephesians:

> *And pray in the Spirit on all occasions with all kinds of prayers and requests. With this in mind, be alert and always keep on praying for all the Lord's people.* (Ephesians 6:18)

There is truly no greater protection of our little ones than that of the spiritual persuasion. The spiritual realm is where we combat Satan, who seeks the harm of our children in every respect. As I have heard it said, "if we win in the Spirit, we win everywhere else."

Despite our best efforts, there will be times where our ability to protect may be limited or insufficient. Jesus's earlier warning intimates the possibility of even his children being led astray. In the times where we are unable to actually keep our children from harm, we naturally want to vindicate them. During the first *Avengers* movie, Tony Stark (aka Iron Man) is confronting the antagonist, Loki, who is leading an alien invasion of Earth with the intent of hostile takeover. As the two exchange banter, Tony says something that captures this feeling so well: "If we can't protect the earth, you can be [darn] well sure we'll avenge it."[37]

Jesus does not take things lying down when someone does harm to one of his little ones. On the contrary, he gives us assurance of his desire and willingness to come to their defense. Not only does this mean dealing with the offender but most importantly ensuring no further harm is done to his child. He continues his discourse in Matthew 18:

> [10]*"See that you do not despise one of these little ones. For I tell you that their angels in heaven always see the face of my Father in heaven.*

---

37   Whedon, J. (Director). (2012). *Marvel's The Avengers* [Motion picture]. USA: Marvel Studios.

[12] "What do you think? If a man owns a hundred sheep, and one of them wanders away, will he not leave the ninety-nine on the hills and go to look for the one that wandered off? [13] And if he finds it, truly I tell you, he is happier about that one sheep than about the ninety-nine that did not wander off. [14] In the same way your Father in heaven is not willing that any of these little ones should perish. (Matthew 18:10-14)

Jesus, being the Good Shepherd, would go to great lengths to ensure the safety of his little ones. He is not satisfied with a near-perfect success rate but leaves the ninety-nine to find the one. In doing so, he emulates the Father in heaven, giving us the perfect example of protection as a father.

As fathers, protection is our calling. It is our responsibility as shepherds of our homes to ensure our children are safe. One of the biggest ways we ensure this safety is by simply being present.

CHAPTER 24:

"ACCESSIBLE"

Traditionally, I can be a pretty hard person to reach.

My friends and family tease me for being the person who never picks up the phone when they call. (If you're reading this, I really am sorry!) It is not so much a matter of not wanting to talk, rather being inaccessible. I may be stepping out on a limb, but I assume most people do not take a phone call from their mom in the middle of a meeting.

We all know what it is like to be unable to speak to someone when they desire to do so. Perhaps you have run into a chatty neighbor while rushing out of the grocery store to a hungry family. Maybe you have even had a salesman knock on the door when you are trying to wrangle your kids for this illusive meal. My favorite is receiving the always untimely call from a telemarketer; not picking up, or hanging up prematurely, probably has more to do with being an unwanted disturbance than anything else.

Busyness as individuals, and as those living in the West, seems to be at an all-time high. Yes, this will mean that we are at times not accessible. We have, though, established how Jesus was busier than anyone that has ever lived (John 21:25). With regards to our children, he models something for us that is all too important:

> [13]*Then people brought little children to Jesus for him to place his hands on them and pray for them. But the disciples rebuked*

them. [14]Jesus said, "Let the little children come to me, and do not hinder them, for the kingdom of heaven belongs to such as these." [15]When he had placed his hands on them, he went on from there. (Matthew 19:13-15)

Honestly, when reading the above passage, I could not help but laugh. This seems like such an innocent scene, with people simply bringing children to Jesus to pray for them. We are all too familiar with the notion of politicians "kissing babies," in an effort to make themselves more appealing as candidates. What I have never seen or heard of is the campaign manager yelling at those unwitting parents and telling them to keep away their kids. Leave it to the disciples to put themselves in this exclusive category.

No, Jesus did not need votes, as God had already selected him to be King. For this reason, maybe the disciples did not see the utility in Jesus being bothered by a group of children? Again, Jesus was busy. He routinely ministered to large crowds and caught the attention, largely negative, of the nation's leading religious authorities. To them, if Jesus was the Messiah, he should have been focusing on building relationships with those in power, not wasting his time with children.

Jesus, however, was known for associating with the lowly. He was not concerned about the haughty, rather the helpless and the humble. In children, then, he finds those who are truly near to his heart. This was so the case, he was willing to rebuke his own disciples for their actions. Not even they would get in the way of the little children coming to him.

Jesus' example speaks to our fatherhood in the following way:

As fathers, we are to be accessible to our children.

Intuitively, this is something we all know. What we also know is how hard it can be to follow through on this. Based on a 2013 Pew Research survey, 53% of all working parents with children under age 18 say it is difficult for them to give attention to both work and family. Subsequently, 46% of fathers conceded feelings of not spending enough time with their children.[38]

As a father, time definitively seems to be the scarcest resource. Despite the expenses surrounding having a baby, we have somehow managed to feed, clothe and care for Marshall thus far in his life. I have commented routinely, though, on how there is not nearly enough time in the day. By the time he is asleep, the laundry list of things to do that day seem to be just as long as when it first began, and I am fortunate to have spent quality time with him. Yes, the weekends typically present a different pace and more opportunity for connection. Weekends, on the other hand, have a different meaning when you're a pastor, with Sundays being a workday and all.

Us dads want the same things. We want our families to be provided for, our homes to have a sense of stability and our lives to have a sense of accomplishment. For many of us, this will mean pursuing meaningful work outside the home. These responsibilities can even, at times, require time and attention in excess of normal office hours. Factor in our kids' school, friends and activities, and there is potential to be ships passing in the night.

Our presence as fathers, nevertheless, must be felt. Truly, there is no replacement for the precious moments our kids can be with us, having our undivided attention. Not only will they feel more connected to us but also have memories of these moments to treasure for the rest of their lives. In order to foster this connection, we will be required to say "no" to some things. This may mean our kids participate in less recreational activities or us even turning down opportunities to advance in our careers that would mean less time with family. As my father-in-law – one of the wisest men I know – says, "every 'yes' to the outside world is a 'no' to your home."

At the very least, we should do our best to arrange our responsibilities to coincide with the family schedule. This, of course, will have some exceptions. Personally, my work requires me to be away from home some

---

38   Modern Parenthood. (2013, September 14). Retrieved September 24, 2020, from https://www.pewsocialtrends.org/2013/03/14/modern-parenthood-roles-of-moms-and-dads-converge-as-they-balance-work-and-family/

weeknights, which essentially means I will not see my little guy before he goes to sleep. In light of this, I try my best to leverage weekday mornings, as I know this will allow for quality time with Marshall. If I am unable to put him down for the night, I can certainly get him when he wakes up.

Writing a book during this season of life has, actually, been very interesting. When I sat down at the onset of this journey, I knew finding time to write was going to be difficult. This would not simply be a matter of scheduling but one of sacrifice, as I would need to make adjustments to my life as a whole in order to accomplish my goal. As a result, many of the pages of this very book have been written in the wee hours of the morning, because of this need to be accessible. Yet, if waking up at 4 a.m. is how I fulfill my calling and serve my family, it is well worth it.

Dad, I know any challenges you are facing with being accessible have nothing to do with desire. You love your children, and I am sure you want to spend all the time with them you can. Often, as you and I can attest, we can feel pulled in two directions. As we have established, Jesus can relate to this.

In the scene we examined, the children are pulling Jesus in one direction and the disciples are pulling him in another. Jesus makes it clear, though, he is never too busy for his little ones. Potentially at the height of his earthly ministry, he stops and gives his attention to these unnamed kids, and we are not given a real reason for their "interruption." While Jairus, the woman with the issue of blood and many others impose on Jesus for very specific reasons, this incident does not seem very purposeful. Perhaps this is exactly the point. When it comes to our children, they do not need to have a "good reason" for coming to us at an untimely moment. Still, they do deserve a response that is "hands on," much like what Jesus demonstrates.

If anyone can make the claim of being busy, it is certainly the President of the United States. Among them, Abraham Lincoln, the nation's 16 president, seemed to have his hands particularly full. He not only was tasked with the Civil War but also the emancipation of African slaves. These two victories perhaps make him the greatest American president, although he was probably most proud to be a dad.

Lincoln had four children, the youngest being named Tad, after Abe's father Thomas. Stories of Tad's antics not only ring through annals of history but also the halls of the White House. He was known to be somewhat of a loose cannon – interesting considering the wartime environment – but was also the life of the house. Since he pretty much had free rein of the house and grounds, he had a penchant for disruption, often finding himself in places you would not expect to see a child. Lincoln's Assistant Secretary of War, Charles A. Dana, details:

> *Often I sat by Tad's father reporting to him about some import-*
> *ant matter that I had been ordered to inquire into, and he would*
> *have this boy on his knee; and, while he would perfectly under-*
> *stand the report, the striking thing about him was his affection*
> *for the child.*[39]

What was in Lincoln's heart for his son is in each of our hearts as fathers. Yes, there will always be the demands of life and vocation that tug at our time and attention. We should convey to our children that there is always room for them. Oftentimes, this will mean saying "no" to things in order to say "yes" to our kids. Interruptions may at times feel inconvenient but can be molded into opportunities for meaningful interaction.

This is the way of Jesus.

When we follow his example, we not only create accessibility for our children but also gain greater access to their hearts. There is perhaps nothing more important for a parent, especially as we aspire to disciple our children.

---

39   Dana, C. A. (1898). *Recollections of the Civil War: With the leaders at Washington and in the field in the sixties*. New York, NY: D. Appleton and Company.

CHAPTER 25:

"FROM THE LIPS OF CHILDREN"

One of my greatest joys thus far as a parent is the satisfaction of knowing I taught Marshall something.

I can recall a time we were sitting in his room reading. He has a great love for balls, and he identified an unfamiliar object on the page as such; honestly, he used to call any and everything a ball. After noticing this, I clarified what he was referencing was a "bubble." It did not take very long for him to adapt this word as part of his growing vocabulary, and I knew it was because of this brief exchange.

One of the main roles of a parent, of a father, is that of a teacher. Currently, we are living in a time where parents are getting more involved in the education of their children, due to the mass migration to the online classroom. While schoolteachers are certainly working hard, it is the parents who are with their kids the entire time they are on the computer. Many of these parents have even opted to homeschool their children, desiring to avoid the amount of screen time and lack of proximity in keeping with remote learning.

Despite this uptick in educational activity and involvement by parents, the truth is we were always responsible for our kids' education. Everything starts with the home, which makes the role of a father so important. As fathers, we have the opportunity to, quite literally, put words in the mouths of our children. It is our responsibility to ensure the words we speak are worth repeating; we never know when our children will parrot them in public.

On one occasion, Jesus experiences a group of children who, undoubtedly, repeat what they heard. Not only did he take notice but also the many who were apart of this scene:

> [14]*The blind and the lame came to him at the temple, and he healed them.* [15]*But when the chief priests and the teachers of the law saw the wonderful things he did and the children shouting in the temple courts, "Hosanna to the Son of David," they were indignant.*
>
> [16]*"Do you hear what these children are saying?" they asked him.*
>
> *"Yes," replied Jesus, "have you never read, 'From the lips of children and infants you, Lord, have called forth your praise'?"*
> (Matthew 21:14-16)

Jesus had entered Jerusalem to begin his last week prior to being crucified. Famously, he rode in on a donkey, signifying his prophetic claim to be King of the Jews. As cloaks and palm branches adorn his triumphal entry, he is met by cries of, "Hosanna to the Son of David" (Matthew 21:9).

As the above passage intimates, he eventually made his way to the temple. The temple was the crowing jewel of the Jews, and it was at the height of activity around the time of the Passover. Jesus entered the temple courts and started to heal the blind and lame; of course, those present could not help but take notice. While the religious establishment was certainly unhappy with Jesus, they became "indignant" when they heard children repeating the words which met him upon his arrival to Jerusalem. When the chief priests and teachers of the law suggest there is something wrong with this scene, Jesus disagrees with them and gives scriptural backing for what the children are saying.

Jesus, quoting from Psalm 8, establishes that God is calling children to praise him. No, this is not something that would only be reserved for adults. On the contrary, from the earliest stages of life, the Great King of all the earth should be acknowledged as such. The children we find in the temple courts are doing as much, having been brought in proximity to the King and repeating what they heard said about him.

Jesus' affirmation of the scene in the temple teaches us the following:

As fathers, we should ensure our children participate in the things of God.

We are all too familiar with the anecdotal Sunday morning scene where the mom is the one getting everyone ready for church. She is waking up the kids, picking out their clothes and reinforcing the imminence of departure, despite their protests. Meanwhile, the dad is removed from the fray and is potentially not even attending with his family, perhaps citing a football game or long week as the reason. Where this scene is a reality, the father is not fulfilling his calling to lead the spirituality of the home.

Jesus believed children should participate in the things of God. He though, was not hands-off regarding their involvement. In fact, he was front and center in the temple, championing worship of God that was inclusive of children. Their presence and participation were validated by his words to those who had even opposed it.

Fathers, the spirituality of our children cannot be left to chance. Our role, then, is to ensure their intentional involvement in things spiritual. This, fundamentally, happens when we ourselves participate and invite them to join us. If we are not, personally, engaging God, we would be remiss to expect our kids to do so.

Typically, when fathers are engaged, the whole family follows suit. In fact, a group of Swiss researchers found that married fathers who regularly attend church were more likely to have children who become regular attendees than fathers who never attended or attended irregularly. Says Robbie Low, English minister and magazine editor, regarding the 1990s study:

In short, if a father does not go to church, no matter how faithful his wife's devotions, only one child in 50 will become a regular worshiper. If a father does go regularly, regardless of the practice of the mother, between two-thirds and three-quarters of their children will become churchgoers.

He adds:

If a father goes but irregularly to church, regardless of his wife's devotion, between a half and two-thirds of their offspring will find themselves coming to church regularly or occasionally.[40]

Moms play such an integral role in the life of the family, the spiritual life in particular. They are often beacons of devotion, and embody a faith worthy of emulation by their children. According to a 2018 Barna Group study, 68 percent of practicing Christians said their faith was influenced by their mother.[41] The devotion of a father, however, is what truly sets the tone for the home. In fact, when the father is the first in the home to become a Christian, there is a 93 percent chance everyone else in the household will follow.[42]

Households that already follow Christ benefit most when dad is leading this spiritual charge. Yes, spiritual leadership can be a daunting task. Jesus, after all, was a master teacher, who was able to refute the top scholars of his day. How can we be teachers of our children when there is so much for us to learn?

While we may not know everything, there is something we can glean from Jesus as we seek to build our kids' faith. On one occasion, he tells

---

40   Gryboski, M. (2019, July 13). Mothers contribute more to kids' spiritual growth than fathers, Barna study says. Retrieved October 05, 2020, from https://www.christianpost.com/news/mothers-contribute-more-kids-spiritual-growth-than-fathers-barna-study.html

41   How Faith Heritage Relates to Faith Practice. (2019, July 9). Retrieved October 06, 2020, from https://www.barna.com/research/faith-heritage-faith-practice/?mc_cid=fc133c2aff

42   House, A., & House, P. (2003, April 3). Want your church to grow? Then bring in the men. Retrieved October 06, 2020, from https://www.baptistpress.com/resource-library/news/want-your-church-to-grow-then-bring-in-the-men/

a parable to a captive audience he is teaching. In it, a farmer goes about sowing seed, which lands on different terrains and produces a crop on the soil deemed good. After leaving the crowd to decipher the meaning of this story for themselves, he privately tells his disciples the meaning, explaining that the seed sown is the word of God (Mark 4:1-20).

Jesus, most certainly, uses the farmer illustration to refer to himself, while there is application for you and me. He knew all there was to know about the Scriptures but when it came time for him to share, he went about it in a way any farmer would: one seed at a time. No, Jesus is not expecting us to write a biblical dissertation to give to our children. Instead, we are to take simple seeds of faith to sow into them. When we sow spiritual seeds in their hearts, they will evidence this by what they say and do.

In watching Marshall grow up, I have been truly amazed at just how much he can absorb – he even speaks another language! Reading, again, is an activity we try to do with him quite regularly. His collection of books is eclectic but he has several of spiritual persuasion. I cannot tell you, though, how many times I have read the same book to him (sometimes in one sitting) and wondered, "Is this really helping?" or "Does he even understand what I'm saying?"

Just when I might be tempted to dismiss the impact of these "seeds," a little sprout appears. No, Marshall may not yet be able to quote a Bible verse verbatim or explain doctrine to someone. Yet, at his young age, he can say the name of "Jesus."

May Jesus' name continue be on his lips, and on those of all our children, as we lead them in the things of God.

CHAPTER 26:

"UNRELENTING"

As a kid, I never really understood the love parents have for their children.

Now being both an adult and a parent, I see that there is truly no love like it. It is fierce, lavish and, at times, even irrational.

My wife loves a movie called, *The Music Man.* In it, a conman posing as a music teacher convinces the parents of an Iowa town to pay for their boys to be a part of a marching band. Intending to skip town prior to the band's debut, he has a change of heart, and is ready to face the music (pun intended) when the parents discern his rouse upon hearing them play. To his surprise, the pride they had in their sons made bad music sound like a beautiful symphony. One mom exclaimed, "Linus, play to me, son!"[43]

I am most amazed, though, by the unrelenting nature of this love. Through thick and thin, parents have a knack for just being there for their kids. Of course, there are exceptions to everything. Where this has been the case, my heart truly goes out to you.

As fathers, committed to the protection, provision and pastoring of our homes, we are to embody this unrelenting love. Of course, it is not always easy. Although, in doing so, we follow in the footsteps of Jesus. In

---

43   DaCosta, M. (Producer), & DaCosta, M. (Director). (1962). *The music man* [Motion picture]. United States: Warner Brothers.

his words to the teachers of the law and Pharisees, he attests to the difficultly of this love:

> *Jerusalem, Jerusalem, you who kill the prophets and stone those*
> *sent to you, how often I have longed to gather your children*
> *together, as a hen gathers her chicks under her wings, and you*
> *were not willing.* (Matthew 23:37)

Jesus, despite the unwillingness of Jerusalem, did not cease in his longing to show these children tender love. This persistence of the Son was not just for the duration of his earthly ministry. In fact, Jesus refers all the way back to Abel's death at the hands of his brother Cain (Matthew 23:35; Genesis 4:8) when noting the stubborn resistance of his people. Their disposition may have been longstanding but so was his love.

Furthermore, having established the reluctance of the scribes and Pharisees to receive God's true messengers, namely himself, he says the following:

> *Therefore I am sending you prophets and sages and teach-*
> *ers. Some of them you will kill and crucify; others you will*
> *flog in your synagogues and pursue from town to town.*
> (Matthew 23:34)

They may not have been listening, but this did not mean he would stop talking. No, Jesus' heart is one of pursuit, desiring to ensure he has used every means to reach those whom he loves. Even after being crucified by this same group of people, he would continue to reach out to them through his followers. Their resistance was likely to persist but the prospect of their repentance made each overture worth it.

Dads, the lesson Jesus teaches us is a tough one, although there is perhaps none more important:

**As fathers, we have to persist in loving our children,
even when they do not want to be loved.**

Have you ever tried to help someone that clearly did not want to be helped? Maybe someone in your life had been experiencing financial hardship yet was unwilling to accept your assistance? More simply, it could even be that you gave a loved one advice that was not received and, certainly, not adhered. I can attest to this in my life.

I am not always the best at receiving advice. Unfortunately, my wife has experienced this more times than desired. On one occasion, I was trying to move an oversized chair from the top floor of our home to the living room, which meant scaling a flight of stairs. Now, the chair had been upstairs since we first moved, and we hired a moving company. Suffice it to say, I had not previously navigated our narrow stairway with the chair.

Heidi, in the most supportive way, suggested I remove the chair legs to help with the transition. Almost immediately, I dismissed her advice and proceeded with my own "plan." Several minutes, contortions and chair scratches later, I found myself adhering to her wise words. If only I had listened to her in the first place.

I am sure each dad has a similar story for their child(ren). Seemingly, our kids have a knack for not listening. While this may be experienced in the vein of advice, this also applies to our holistic desire to parent them. Our words of instruction and even affection can, at times, be dismissed. We, still, should not be discouraged, as this places us in the company of one another and of Christ.

Jesus knows what it is like to not be received (John 1:11). He had left his place in heaven, in the greatest gesture of pursuit, but was largely unwanted. For this reason, he was a man of sorrows (Isaiah 53:3). He was not, however, a man of self-pity or of bitterness but continued to love until the very end. In fact, his death was an expression of his love. Paul writes, "But God demonstrates his own love for us in this: While we were still sinners, Christ died for us" (Romans 5:8).

As we have noted, even death would not stop his unrelenting love. After Jesus rose from the grave, he sought the people who denied, denounced and decimated him. We might not have been there during his lifetime but by virtue of our sin, we are all collaborators with this group. Oh, what love he expresses to each of us, as he has pursued us into relationship with himself!

Dads, when we ourselves feel as if we are not being received, it is the love of Christ that compels us to persist in loving our children. The love needed during these times, however, may be of the "tough" persuasion. There is always a place for kisses, hugs and words of affirmation – we should, indeed, love our kids affectionately. Where this persistence is needed, though, at least two other things will be strategically employed: *discipline* and *patience*.

We have, previously, discussed discipline in brief. Since it is such a vital facet of our roles as fathers, it is worthy of being revisited. Yes, it is how we train, reinforce and protect; this also amounts to how we express love. As Proverbs 3:12 says, "the LORD disciplines those he loves, as a father the son he delights in."

Jesus was a man committed to correction. The earlier quotes from Matthew 23 are mere snippets of an at-length rebuke of the scribes and Pharisees known as the "Seven Woes." While this group may be considered Jesus' opponents, they are certainly not peers, identifying them in his address as part of the people historically categorized as the children of Jerusalem. To these people, God had sent many prophets to issue words of admonishment but was now doing so in the person of Jesus (Hebrews 1:1-2).

Just as Jesus made a commitment to persist in correction, we must do the same: this requires patience. Things may seem tough for a while but discipline over time will yield a harvest of righteousness in our children. Yes, this entails willful action on our part. Sometimes, though, we do this through inaction, as we allow consequences to take shape in our children's lives. Just ask Pastor Jim.

Pastor Jim Cymbala is the leader of the Brooklyn Tabernacle, a world-renowned megachurch in Brooklyn, NY known for its emphasis on prayer and the ministry of its 300-voice choir. He and his wife, Carol, took over the church in 1971 and have since seen tremendous spiritual fruit.

Their oldest daughter, Chrissy, invited Jesus into her heart when she was five years old. While she was sincere in this profession and faithful in attending church, her teenage years saw her being more attracted to the things of the world. Soon, Chrissy would distance herself from the church, her parents and even God. The result was being found with child as a young, unmarried woman.

She lived with her parents for a time, but it became clear they would not be able to co-exist. Chrissy moved out and would need to fend for herself with her new daughter. On one occasion, when things were particularly difficult, she recalls going to her parents' house to manipulate her way back home. To her surprise, her knock at the door was unanswered. As Chrissy sat shocked in her car, her mom later came out to greet her new granddaughter and clarify that they had drawn a hard line with her; her dad would not even see her.

As I reflect on this story, the unanswered knock at the door was the most loving thing Chrissy's dad could have done for her. She needed to reach the end of her rope, and this would only happen if he did not come to the rescue. Sure enough, things did take a turn in her life. In a fated prayer meeting, the church prayed for Chrissy's return, which materialized in a matter of hours. (You can find the full story in Chrissy's book, "Girl in the Song.")

Dads, God ultimately does the work but calls on us to lay the groundwork of persistent love, especially when it is difficult.

As I was doing research on this topic, my heart was saddened to hear of instances where fathers were unable to do this. One time in particular involved an unwed 17-year-old who was found to be with child. Upon sharing the news of her pregnancy with her father, Joe, an avid churchgoer, he retorted:

> *How could you do this to me? You know how I've tried to raise you, and look what you've done!*

He adds:

> *You listen to me. I don't want this baby, and I don't want you. Get your things together and leave right now! Don't ever set foot in this house again. Do you understand me?*[44]

I can only imagine how painful those words were to hear; they were painful to write. Joe probably felt he had been rejected. His efforts to instill a moral compass into this young lady were, perhaps, viewed as completely ignored. His unwillingness to love her through this, in the end, forfeited an opportunity to influence the rest of her and her child's lives. As a result, this young lady has experienced several failed marriages, feeling far away from her father and God.

This was not tough love, rather the lack thereof. In juxtaposing Joe's response and Pastor Cymbala's, we see the difference between *correction* and *rejection*. One has *learning* has the end, the other *leaving*. Both daughters left, sure enough, but only one daughter's return was desired.

The love Jesus embodies always desires a return, no matter how far his children have strayed. In fact, his contemporaries had gotten so far from God, they did not recognize him when he showed up to talk to them. Nevertheless, he continued the conversation, and pursued them even beyond being crucified.

When we love like this, we not only look like Jesus but also leave a legacy of love to be passed on to our children's children. What better thing is there for us to leave behind?

---

44   Waldrep, P. (2019, February 01). A Story of Two Prodigals. Retrieved October 16, 2020, from https://www.familylife.com/articles/topics/parenting/parenting-challenges/anger-and-rebellion/a-story-of-two-prodigals/

CHAPTER 27:

"WHEN I'M GONE"

One of the most sobering things about fatherhood is realizing you will not always be there for your kids.

Yes, you will try to be there for every game, recital and important milestone. Based on the natural order of things, though, there will come a day when our children have to tell us, "goodbye." If you're like me, just reading this makes you tear up a bit.

When I think of little Marshall and all of the life ahead of him, I cannot imagine missing any part of it. From graduations, to his wedding day, to his first child, there are so many things to look forward to in his life; although, I would not be heartbroken if I missed out on potty training and him learning how to drive. Still, it would be unreasonable for me to deny the eventuality of my departure, also conceding the uncertainty of this timeline. As much as I want to be in the present with him, I would be remiss to not think about the future.

In addressing his disciples, Jesus conveys this fatherly sentiment. John records his words as follows:

> ³³*My children, I will be with you only a little longer. You will look for me, and just as I told the Jews, so I tell you now: Where I am going, you cannot come.* ³⁴*A new command I give you:*

Love one another. As I have loved you, so you must love one another. [35]By this everyone will know that you are my disciples, if you love one another. (John 13:33-35)

Jesus addressed his disciples in a lot of ways. He called them brothers (Matthew 12:49), friends (John 15:15) and even those of little faith (Matthew 8:26). How fitting is it that he also identifies them as his "children."

In John's gospel, we are given a more intimate access to Jesus' final moments prior to crucifixion than the other gospel writers. For instance, in John 17, as Jesus is likely praying in Gethsemane, we find his longest prayer on record. It follows, then, how John captures this cherished moment between Jesus and the disciples, this being the only place in the gospels where he addresses them as his kids. He had watched them grow up for the past three years, and now he would be leaving them.

I imagine this being an emotional conversation for Jesus. For most people, their transition from this life is unknown. To sit across from those whom you raised and tell them you will only be alive for "a little longer" certainly does not seem enjoyable. As always, Jesus deals in the truth, telling the disciples plainly about his departure. In fact, they later commented, "Now you are speaking clearly and without figures of speech" (John 16:29).

Through the experiences of others, I know there have been times where a parent has hidden a terminal illness. Quite obviously, this never ends well. Death is, of course, the unfortunate result, barring divine intervention. Keeping it a secret does not allow loved ones to prepare for what will seem to them sudden. When it comes to this aspect of life, transparency is always best.

While our children should be able to prepare for this moment, most important is us making preparations for them. Jesus knew this and embodied this aspect of fatherhood in addressing his disciples. What we learn from him, then, is this:

As fathers, we need to prepare
our children for when we're gone.

This is something we all know but is so helpful to keep in front of us. We have each been called to live purposefully in our time on this earth. By virtue of having children, though, this is to extend even beyond our lifetime.

Generally, when we think of this, things like life insurance, trust funds and inheritances come to mind. These things are important, as we are certainly to pass on to our children what we have amassed in our lifetime. Maybe you are reading this and saying to yourself, "I don't have anything to give." My friend, everybody has something, and as sure as God has entrusted us with our children, he has given us the means to bless them. "Houses and wealth are inherited from fathers" (Proverbs 14:19a ESV) but everything comes from the Lord.

Jesus, himself, did not neglect this responsibility. In fact, he continues his conversation with the disciples by saying:

> [1]*Do not let your hearts be troubled. You believe in God; believe also in me.* [2]*My Father's house has many rooms; if that were not so, would I have told you that I am going there to prepare a place for you?* [3]*And if I go and prepare a place for you, I will come back and take you to be with me that you also may be where I am.* (John 14:1-3)

The disciples were assured that Jesus had something prepared *for* them. He, of course, thought this was significant enough to mention although not as a matter of first importance. Jesus was preparing the place but this place would be in the "Father's house" – again, everything comes from him. Of greatest concern to Jesus was not what they would be left but the condition in which he would leave them. This is why he addresses his departure and their character in the same breath.

If you have read any portion of this book, you know that I am a Marvel© movie enthusiast. This lesson makes me think of one of my favorite films,

Black Panther. The main character, T'Challa, has been recently crowned king of Wakanda after his father, T'Chaka, tragically died in an explosion. After undergoing a series of African rituals as part of his installation, he visits the mystical ancestral plane, where he is able to communicate with past kings. Seeing his father, the two have a brief, yet emotional exchange:

> *T'Challa: "I am not ready to be without you."*
>
> *T'Chaka: "A man who has not prepared his children for his own death has failed as a father."*[45]

While T'Chaka's words are strong, they do stress the significance of a father's role in the development of a child and the limited time in which to do so. He left T'Challa an inheritance sure enough. Had he not taught him the lessons necessary to prepare him to rule, however, leaving behind the commodities of the kingdom would have been in vain. Perhaps this is why Solomon addresses the Proverbs, by-in-large, to his son. We may expire but the lessons we teach our children will remain in their hearts and minds. It is absolutely imperative that we sow all the seeds of preparation we can now, because there will come a time where we can no longer do so.

While this education should certainly be intentional, you cannot expect every learning moment to be scripted. Sometimes, opportunities will arise to sow seed in the hearts of our children just based on circumstance. Other times, this will just happen as a result of us living our lives.

Again, my father was not around as a kid but I did experience this with my grandfather, Willie Dorsey. I was frequently in my grandparents' home, so we spent a lot of time together. One time, when it was just the two of us, we were sitting at the kitchen table where he was eating cereal, which he often did. This time, I noticed that he said a prayer before he ate. My family always made it a habit of praying before meals but in my mind, this was something reserved for "big meals," not bowls of cereal. When

---

45   Coogler, R. (Director). (2019). *Black panther* [Motion picture]. Milano: Walt Disney Studios home entertainment.

I asked him about it, he explained how we should give thanks to God for everything. Sure enough, I have been giving thanks for bowls of cereal and whatever else since this day.

Dad, do not doubt the power of a moment! There will be occasions where an exchange you think is rather mundane is easily recalled by your children years later. I was impacted by a bowl of cereal; your children may remember helping you with a project or going with you to work. Jesus was the master of maximizing moments, and the night of the Passover was no exception.

Jesus knew he would rise from the grave and even spend 40 more days with his disciples (Acts 1:3). Still, he did not want to forfeit this opportunity to carry on his legacy through his spiritual children. This was not a legacy of success or fame but one of love. If they were going to rule in his stead, carrying on his kingdom movement, they would have to do so like he did; this was to be demonstrated, first, amongst themselves.

In order to best prepare his children to be without him, Jesus knew he had to drive home "love." This was not the conditional love with which they had been familiar but the self-sacrificing love he exemplified in washing their feet and, eventually, dying on the cross. Doing so not only created a healthier dynamic amongst a group that had previously sought to secure their own kingdom positions but also established a culture that would be passed on for generations.

While our time may be limited, each day affords us an opportunity to prepare our kids for the future. There are so many things to navigate in this world. Now saying, "follow me as I follow Christ," will enable our children to follow Christ even when our race has ended. I know it is a sad thought, but I cannot imagine there being a better feeling for a father than knowing your child is ready to stand on his or her own.

Our role in our children's lives never is obsolete although it does evolve as they grow. Even in my short time of parenting, I have watched Marshall become less dependent on me. While I used to have to carry him everywhere, he now wants to walk on his own. Though he used to need me to feed him his bottle, he now opens the refrigerator and makes selections for himself (oftentimes, this results in things being returned). Yes, things have changed but it makes me no less his father; on the contrary, it actually makes me proud.

Fatherhood is a road littered with emotions. To start the journey raising someone so dependent on you, only to realize you are to actively help them depend on you less, can be challenging. It is coming to terms with our mortality, though, which allows us to focus on the task at hand. When our time to transition comes, I pray we will be able to echo these words of Christ concerning his children:

> [6]*I have revealed you to those whom you gave me out of the world. They were yours; you gave them to me and they have obeyed your word.* [7]*Now they know that everything you have given me comes from you.* [8]*For I gave them the words you gave me and they accepted them.* (John 17:6-8a)

Dads, let us stand with Jesus and raise up our sons and daughters, revealing to them the glory of the Father. His legacy is, ultimately, what will last.

CONCLUSION

Each of us has probably been to a funeral at one point or another.

While funerals are typically times of sadness, they also serve as a time of reflection. Of course, everyone is thinking about the life of the deceased. This will either be a life well-lived or one full of regret. How tragic it is when the latter is the case.

What we remember most fondly of the people who have run their race well is not how much money they earned or how many properties they owned but the impact they made on others. These are those whose spouses, children, relatives and friends speak of them most highly. Story after story is told of what made this individual so special to the people saying their goodbyes.

It is not just the life of the person in the casket we are thinking about, though. At a certain point, their race starts to make us think of our own. Hearing of the footsteps of another, especially the missteps, has a tendency to make us more calculated. Inevitably, I find myself asking the question, "What will people say about me at my funeral?"

In the end, we each want to be able to say with Paul, "I have fought the good fight, I have finished the race, I have kept the faith" (1 Timothy 4:7). Our daily resolve to emulate Jesus is what truly makes this possible. Our journeys are circuitous, demanding and unpredictable. Running an amazing race is predicated on following the path of the one who has perfectly navigated the course.

Here then is an encouragement from the writer of Hebrews:

And let us run with endurance the race God has set before us. [2]We do this by keeping our eyes on Jesus, the champion who initiates and perfects our faith. (Hebrews 1b-2a NLT)

Our race does require endurance but it is one Jesus will help us to complete. He has provided for us an amazing example. All we have to do is run with it.